Modern
Development
in Yacht
Design

David Cannell and John Leather

Modern
Development
in Yacht
Design

Dodd, Mead & Company/New York

Published in the United States of America 1976
by Dodd, Mead & Company, Inc.

First published in Great Britain 1976 by Adlard Coles Limited

Copyright © 1976 by David Cannell and John Leather

ISBN: 0-396-07355-7
Library of Congress Catalog Card Number: 76-11397
Printed in Great Britain

Contents

Acknowledgements

The authors are grateful to Roger Bell, of David M Cannell, Naval Architects, for his patient help with the illustrations, and to Kirin Davids and Jackie Maynard for typing the manuscript.

Introduction

What types of yacht will be popular in the 1980s? How will they differ from today's craft? How will yachting develop?

This book attempts to answer these questions because there is little doubt that the future decade promises to be one of the most exciting in the sport's history. The dramatic increase in the popularity of sailing during the last fifteen years will be sustained together with the technical and social changes that have already created new areas of interest for everyone involved.

One theme of the book is that little sense can be made of the future without an understanding of how the present situation has been reached. Thus, the chapters dealing with specific yacht types (Chapters 2, 3 and 4) spend some time discussing the history of the craft so that development can be put in its proper context.

The subsequent chapters deal with the development of yacht components ranging over masts, spars, rig and sails in Chapter 5, engines and powering in Chapter 6, materials and construction in Chapter 7 and interior design in Chapter 8.

The opening chapter looks at the general situation, indicating developments in the sport as a whole which will affect yacht design and the methods of participation in sailing in the future.

1
The future

Each year more and more people participate in the art of sailing. There are many reasons for this, including changing leisure patterns, the desire 'to get away from it all', the relative decrease in the cost of sailing resulting from the mass production of boats and equipment, and increased affluence. There is little need to question whether this trend will continue. The important issue is to see how the sailing world will adapt to make room for its new recruits.

The first problem to be overcome is that of overcrowding. During recent years the development of the marina has made it possible for many more people to enjoy sailing from one local base. At times the marina will create overcrowded situations which can make the return to port on a Sunday evening almost as bad as the crawl back by car on the roads. However, the proportion of boats which put to sea only two or three times a year has been estimated to be as high as 60 per cent. Some boats do not leave their berths at all except for a mid-summer scrub off! Of course, this does not mean that such boats are not used. Many people spend a pleasant day visiting their craft, doing odd jobs aboard and pottering around without actually taking the boat out. It follows, therefore, that the marina has the capacity for a fairly dense population of boats with great advantages over traditional moorings in estuaries and rivers.

Rivers and estuaries can neither cope with future growth nor offer the advantages of better toilet facilities and other services which are catered for in marina design. Sometimes the development of a large marina may not be possible as it might spoil the natural beauty of an area. When this occurs it is suggested that river and estuary moorings should be reserved for day boats and small one-design racers allowing cabin boats and cruisers to berth in a small marina.

Dry marinas, which operate rather like multi-storey car parks, will be a future development allowing storage space ashore for hundreds of craft up to about 35 ft long. Smaller boats will be placed in two-tier racks served by fork-lift trucks, the larger boats in cradles; all will be launched and recovered on a ramp. The dry system, already in use with small keel boats such as Flying 15s, would increase the cost of yachting as boat handling charges will accelerate. Offset against this, however, will be the elimination of the cost of stagings and pontoons of the usual marina.

The increase in the number of people sailing will put pressure on coastal waterways in Europe. It is to be expected, therefore, that there will be greater use of Continental inland waterways not only by the people through whose countries they run, but also by the large number of holiday-makers from Britain and North America seeking an unusual cruising ground surrounded by a countryside abounding in historical associations. To cater for this, the concept of the 'boatel' will be further developed. Set at planned intervals along the European waterway systems, the boatels will enable hirers to use specially designed inland water cruising craft of modest size which will accommodate up to eight people, with ample cockpit observation space and a day cabin with cooking facilities and other necessary services. Co-operation among the owners of these craft would enable the hirer to leave his boat at the boatel of his choosing allowing him more time to sail through new waters without retracing a route back to the starting point.

In line with the development of the marina and the boatel will be the development of mobile sailing bases. It is to be expected that, as shore site facilities become more difficult to obtain, growing numbers of clubs and class associations will own mobile sailing base vessels, the more sophisticated of which will be capable of making coastal passages. They will be equipped with starting platform, changing rooms, toilets, showers and a large deckhouse for use as a committee or race briefing room. The base ship will also be capable of use as a racing base, carrying perhaps a dozen small keel boats or correspondingly more smaller centre-boarders, in a sort of floating dock, with the after end flooded, enabling the boats to enter and leave through a stern gate. When the stern gate is closed the space can be pumped dry to make something like a landing-ship dock.

The advantage of all this is that a small fleet of one-design boats could be transported around the coast to a series of fixtures, using the same craft for the selection of national or international champions, or to vary a club's racing venues throughout the season. It is probable that these mobile bases will be new clubs in themselves rather than extensions of existing organisations. The broadest development of the concept would have cabin or open-plan accommodation for the crews of all boats carried, with the necessary galley and catering space, besides live-aboard accommodation for its own crew. There will be a hydraulic crane capable of lifting for repair the larger type of boat carried, and also able to step masts, and load equipment. The initial investment in such a ship, at present estimated at about £200,000, seems quite reasonable with a life expectancy of 40 years and, besides having the advantage of mobility, it compares favourably with the cost and difficulty of obtaining waterside club premises in popular yachting areas.

The rising costs of yacht construction will encourage widespread development of 'boatbuilding clubs', and of firms offering specialist services. These services will include building, equipment, materials, supply and, if necessary, skilled assistance in laying off lines and making templates, or indeed in any stage of construction. Foam core sandwich plastic,

steel and ferrocement will be the major materials catered for in this way, but wood and aluminium alloy will be preferred by some.

Boatbuilding clubs will offer bulk purchase of materials and fittings, particularly for a number of craft of the same design. A fixed sum paid by each club member into a common fund before construction starts will provide a sound financial foundation for purchasing. Incremental payments will be added to this as the work progresses. The success of such schemes will depend on the Secretary who will be the key man in such enterprises. He will need a sound knowledge of purchasing practice and, of course, the kind of tact and patience necessary to deal with members all impatient to get their dream ships launched.

Rising costs will encourage not only the formation of boatbuilding clubs but also an interest in amateur building of small craft and cruising yachts. Plywood is the usual material for amateurs, but ferrocement will increase in appeal despite the difficulties of its construction.

The expansion of the sport of sailing will see a continuing increase in the number of young sailors afloat. Thus, there will be an increase in the number of sail-training craft and youth organisations taking boys and girls to sea. Development here will see international racing in square-riggers manned by large crews of young people. These larger craft do have the disadvantage, however, that there is little opportunity for everyone involved to have a fair trick at the wheel or to plot a course for a day's passage and to understand what he is doing. The costs of such craft are high and may be well beyond the reach of even large youth clubs. Consequently, there is a demand for a good 40-ft boat with limited draught but a good spread of sail. Training yachts of this type could be moulded in GRP, and taken from the same parent form enabling an 'international

Fig. 1.1. Profile of a 150-ft racing schooner. Suitable for true ocean racing, craft of this type could be expected to attain 20 knots off the wind.

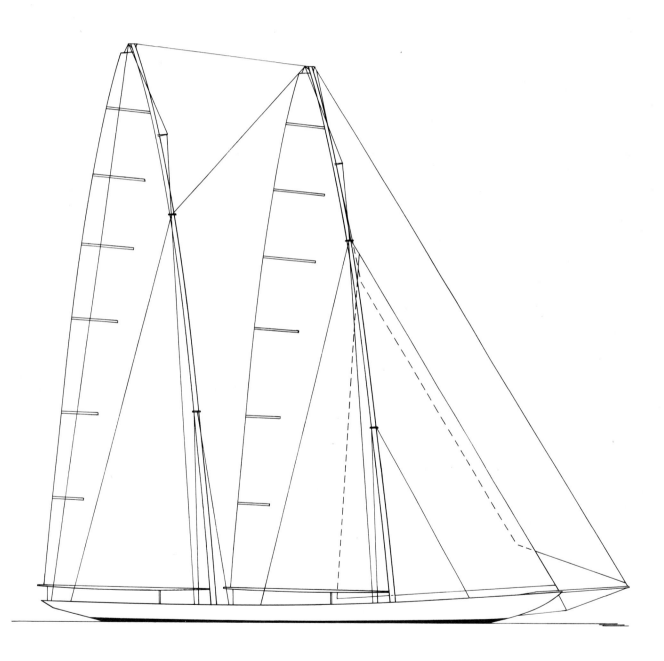

youth one-design' to be created. Racing between clubs of different countries owning these craft could be arranged, thus encouraging enthusiasm for maintaining the club boat to a good standard, as well as developing the competitive ability of the crews.

Single-handed ocean racing will steadily increase its appeal although it will still be undertaken by a small group of people. Here one can expect, without the restrictions of artificial rating rules, the design of easily handled sailing yachts. Such yachts will tend to represent the best in ocean sailing practice more truly than the more intensively developed offshore racing craft, in which strength and ease of handling are often discounted against good rescue facilities and large crews.

As an extension to offshore racing the development of very large sailing yachts for long-distance racing will be seen. This will be true ocean racing, probably crewed from the Armed Services and similar organisations where a high level of physical attainment is encouraged. These craft (Fig. 1.1) could be 150 ft long, with crews of 20 to 30, and setting up to 12,000 sq ft of canvas in ketch or schooner rigs; craft reminiscent of the large inshore racing yachts of the past. These larger *New Endeavours* could be used for racing and cruising throughout their lives thus comparing favourably with the modern 12-Metre, that overgrown day boat, which spends much of its life laid up ashore. Furthermore, their appearance on the scene would greatly enliven public interest in such races as the America's Cup which, at the moment, require an enormous investment in the pursuit of small technical advances because of the restrictions of an old-fashioned rating rule.

Other exciting developments in the types of yacht being built will centre probably on the small hovercraft and the hydrofoil. The hovercraft and hydrofoil are being used commercially with great success at the moment because they offer a fast and comfortable passage. Various navies have also been carrying out trials and developments; for instance, HMCS *Bras d'Or* exceeds 60 knots in smooth water with a 200-ton displacement.

2

The sailing yacht

Sailing yachts became popular in the early nineteenth century when their hull forms and rigs were derived from fast commercial and naval craft. Long straight keels, plumb stems, short counter sterns and beautiful sections were characteristic of their ancestry.

After the 1830s, racing became established and allowances for differences in size soon evolved into early rating rules. The best remembered of these is the Thames Measurement Tonnage rule which had its origins in the tonnage of merchant ships and is still used, although officially discarded in 1874, as a measurement of comparison by British yachtsmen.

The rule,* with breadth as the principal variable, made increases in breadth lead to great increases in rating. This influenced the building of narrower and deeper craft than the more shapely early forms. Depth was further exaggerated at the expense of breadth since all ballast was carried within the hull. Thus, to achieve the necessary righting moment for the tons of lead fitted in the bottom, the hulls had to be deeper still.

This development reached a climax in the 1880s when some racing yachts were built with a breadth of only one-sixth of their length. And when, in 1878, tonnage length was measured on the waterline, plumb stems were replaced by graceful clipper bows creating controversy about their 'ugliness'. The story of the 5-tonner *Oona* built at Wivenhoe in 1886 shows most tragically the freakish effect of the breadth-inhibiting rating rule. Designed by the talented young William Payton, she had only a 5-ft-6-in beam, a 33-ft-10-in waterline, yet drew 8 ft. Her displacement was 12·5 tons of which her lead keel was 9·6 tons. Her construction was very light with double skin planking on steel frames and she set 2000 sq ft of working canvas. The *Oona* was lost with all hands on passage off the Irish coast. That same year the Clyde 3-tonners carried the rule to even more ridiculous extremes, having a 29-ft water line and 4-ft-6-in beam with enormous lead keels and huge sail areas.

In 1887 the introduction of the new rule,† with its emphasis on length and sail area, brought a revival to racing which had stagnated under the earlier excesses. All classes of British racing yachts were affected – from tiny ½-raters to 151-raters such as *Britannia*, *Valkyrie*, *Calluna* and *Satanita*. In America too there was a reawakened interest and craft from cup defenders to canoes were being designed, built and sailed throughout the country. Thus the 1890s became one of the great periods of the racing sailing yacht. Magnificent boats like the *Britannia* and her contemporaries in America had light displacement, useful and graceful overhangs, speed-developing rigs and sensible accommodation. And the smaller classes, from ½- to 5-rating, displayed so much originality in experimental hull form that by the end of the century they had reached, and in many cases exceeded, the small ballast keel profile and skeg, or independently mounted rudders, of present-day yachts. Their displacement for principal dimensions was far less though sail areas were considerably greater. Their speed, even though they may not have pointed so high going to windward, was greater than that of the craft we sail today. No pretence was made to provide accommodation, these classes being regarded only as dayboats.

Despite the success of this rule, it was inevitable, to avoid excess, evasion and stagnation, that further changes should take place to maintain life in the

$$* \text{ Rating} = \frac{L \times B \times B/2}{94} = \frac{L \times B^2}{188},$$
where L is length, B is breadth, B/2 is depth.

$$† \frac{L \times \text{Sail Area}}{6000} = 1000$$

Fig. 2.1. Sections of early racing yachts. The rating rules at that time penalised beam but not draught – here the 'plank on edge' type, of which *Oona* was an extreme example.

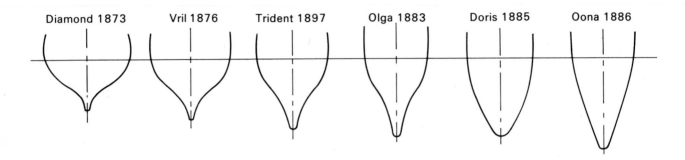

Diamond 1873   Vril 1876   Trident 1897   Olga 1883   Doris 1885   Oona 1886

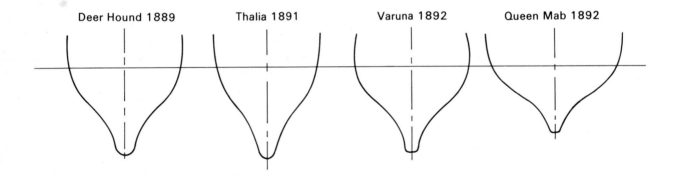

Deer Hound 1889   Thalia 1891   Varuna 1892   Queen Mab 1892

sport. The linear rating rule which followed in 1896 produced yachts rated in feet of which the 52-footers were most popular, having developed out of the earlier 20-raters, and 20-tonners.

In 1907 a new rule was conceived which was to dominate yacht racing in Europe and Scandinavia for thirty years, and lingers on in the 5·5-Metres, 6-Metres and 12-Metres today. The formation of the International Yacht Racing Union was unfortunately not supported by American yachtsmen, who decided in favour of their own Universal Rule. Thus an opportunity was lost for stimulating development to mutual advantage. For over a century British yachtsmen have been greatly interested in any development of racing hulls, rigs or equipment from across the Atlantic; a fascination which shows no signs of diminishing.

The International Rating classes produced by this European rule were rated in metres, and until 1914 very large numbers of 6-, 8-, 12- and 15-Metre yachts were built and lesser numbers of 7, 10, 19-Metres and yachts of 23-Metres and above. These boats were concentrated in Britain, Scandinavia and Europe, particularly in Germany where since about 1890 the sport of sailing in craft of every size, and especially dinghies and other small boats, had been given every possible encouragement. The rule to which these new yachts were built was intended to promote stronger construction and encourage useful post-racing lives as cruising yachts, even if this sacrificed some of the speed of the preceding types.

While the hulls were developing in an extreme manner, rigs were rapidly tending to increase the height and shorten the base of the sail plan, a process which was begun during the 1890s. The 15-Metre *Istria* of 1911 stepped a lower mast and topmast in one, with the traditional topsail yard abolished and the luff of a triangular topsail set to the topmast on a track. This Marconi rig was a forerunner of Bermudian rig in larger classes, but as ever the small boats were ahead.

Bermudian rig is a development of a triangular type of sail which was in use in Bermuda, among other places, at the beginning of the nineteenth century, was also set in other craft, particularly ships' boats, and had been used in Holland in earlier times. Like the small raters, small-metre boats at first set very high-peaked lugsails which were almost triangular in shape. In 1911 the 6-Metre *Gypateos* was designed by G. U. Laws, one of the most brilliant English yacht designers, whose name is now almost unknown. She set a Bermudian mainsail on a track and its success was quickly imitated by many other small-class boats in Britain and Europe, although Bermudian rig was not fitted in a large racer until *Nyria* was thus rerigged for the 1921 season. About that time, Bermudian rig appeared on the British-owned 12-Metre *Noreen* and, after a few masts had

been lost it gained steady development in that class. In 1926 Fife designed the large racing yacht *Cambria* for Bermudian rig, which within five years dominated large-class racing.

In 1929 the Americans agreed to adopt the International Yacht Racing Union rules for classes below 15-Metres, and Britain agreed to adopt the American Universal Rule for larger yachts, which brought the big class from the metre rating to a J rating, thus permitting competition and development between the large racers of the two countries and stimulating challenges for the America's Cup.

Although the IYRU rules were modernised during the 1920s and 1930s, interest in the metre classes was restricted to a circle of yachtsmen devoted to day racing. However, from small beginnings in the late 1920s, the sport of racing cruising yachts on a handicap formula over courses alongshore and occasionally on passages offshore, grew rapidly in Britain, Europe and North America following the pattern set largely by the efforts of Thomas Fleming Day. In 1906 this American had instituted racing from Newport to Bermuda with a view to improving the seaworthiness of cruising yachts and the seamanship of their amateur crews.

Offshore racing grew as rapidly in Britain and Europe as it had earlier in America, leading during the 1930s to the formulation of sound rules which produced many yachts of great beauty and excellence. This trend continued after 1945, modified by changes in keeping with the smaller yachts forced on British and American yachtsmen by economic circumstances. Since then, offshore yachts have developed gradually to a pitch of machine-like complexity and, in general, have long abandoned the healthy intentions of the original rule makers. However, the development of craft able to carry their sail area to windward in strong winds and considerable seas has been maintained, though their

Plate 1. *American Eagle*, now racing as a Class 1 offshore racer although designed under the 12-Metre Rule, is still competitive in offshore racing, particularly in windward sailing. *Photo:* Beken

spartan accommodation cannot house comfortably their large crews.

The brief survey above shows how yacht design had been affected by rating rules. When looking at the future the effect of the International Offshore Rule will be ignored for the most part since it is strongly suggested that designers should pay less attention to getting round the rule and more to the production of sound fast craft. This would benefit offshore racing to a marked degree. The history of the 12-Metre *American Eagle* shows that a well-designed hull shape, although having a poor rating, can compete successfully with lighter, modern vessels built to the offshore rule.

The pattern of the past indicates that the present offshore racing machine must give way to a more useful yacht in the future.

One may expect a longer and narrower yacht, manned by a smaller crew and capable of higher speeds to windward and reaching, with headsail areas restricted and mainsails of useful area and reasonable proportions. The accommodation will probably be more rigidly controlled by a rule requiring not only sufficient bunks and toilet facilities for the crew, but also a galley having the capacity to cook meals for the total complement at one time, backed up by minimum scales of stores which must be carried on board at the start of a race related to each member of the crew and the normally anticipated duration of the longest race in which yachts of that class will participate. This will ensure that designers must provide sufficient displacement for a healthy racer-cruiser.

A further development to reduce costs will be the construction of one-design hulls for series production of offshore yachts. Although static in hull design and development, these will encourage better seamanship, crewing, helmsmanship and navigation; and to some extent rig development.

There is still room for moderately proportioned hull forms in modern racing. This is proved by the performance of the long-keel, slack-bilge hull form which the 12-Metre rating rule encourages by its girth measurement. These types have the advantage that the hull has a very low wetted surface area, which has a major effect at low speeds where skin fraction is of prime importance. The hard bilge has its merits in giving a high initial stability, thus benefiting windward work in medium airs. The righting moment of these two hull forms are compared (Fig. 2.2). Thus, in the design of the racing sailing yacht we are juggling with two important features each of which has its merits. The fin and skeg racing yacht achieves both a hard-bilge and low-wetted surface area by cutting away a large proportion of keel, as can be seen by the profile drawings (Fig. 2.3). It was realised, much to many designers' amazement, that leeway did not suddenly increase when the area of keel was reduced by removing the section between the fin and the rudder. This had long been accepted by model yacht-racing enthusiasts, and the designer of today's offshore racing yacht would do well to consider closely the hull forms and development of model yachts.

In the future far more thought will be given to the design of the drop-keel racing yacht because of the very great importance of the effect of wetted surface area on speed in light winds. Hull form becomes the main consideration when the speed/length ratio $V/\sqrt{L}$ reaches say 0·9. If the wave form of a deep, long-keeled boat is studied when it is moving at its maximum speed, the wave length is found to run along the waterline as shown in Fig. 2.4. This wave becomes deeper if more bulk of boat is present around amidships. Thus the answer to both the wetted surface and the hull resistance effects is to alter the keel configuration according to the sailing conditions. Off the wind in heavy weather, without a

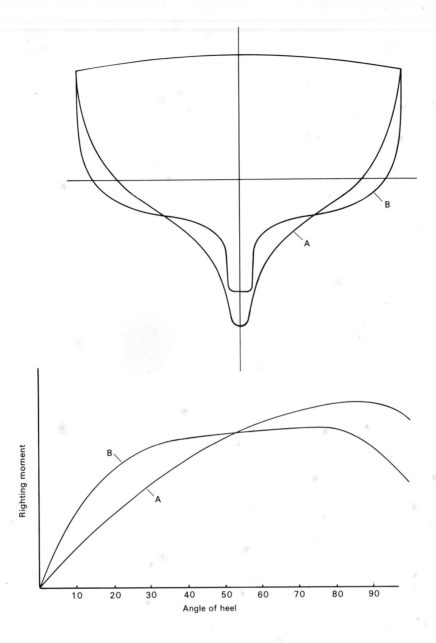

keel present, the sailing yacht would more readily lift and start to plane, thus overcoming the wave resistance problem. Quite obviously the main difficulty in producing a drop-keel offshore racing hull is stability. Although heeling would be considerably reduced without a keel because the lateral resistance is decreased, with the keel raised the ultimate stability is reduced and capsizing or broaching is possible. The method of overcoming this is shown in Fig. 2.5. The underwater hull form consists of a torpedo-shape lead ballast keel attached to the hull by steel girders along the centreline, forming a channel, and some hydrodynamically

shaped rods to stabilise the keel running up to the bilge. Down the channel on the centreline a drop plate can be lowered, thus reducing leeway and increasing wetted surface as required. When going to windward in all but very heavy conditions the drop plate would be fully lowered, and though off the wind the plate would be fully raised, the stability would be in no way impaired as the main ballast has not been moved. In very heavy conditions the drop plate is partially raised to reduce heeling moment.

The centreline keel yacht does not offer maximum leeway resistance when heeled as some water will flow under the keel. Thus the keel is inefficient in

Fig. 2.2 (*left*). Sections of two hull forms and chart of righting moments. The form with the hard bilge has a greater initial stability but at angles of heel of 50° or more the slack-bilged deeper-keeled type has greater stability.

Fig. 2.3. Hull profiles through the ages. It has been found that a reduction in lateral area need not be detrimental to windward performance.

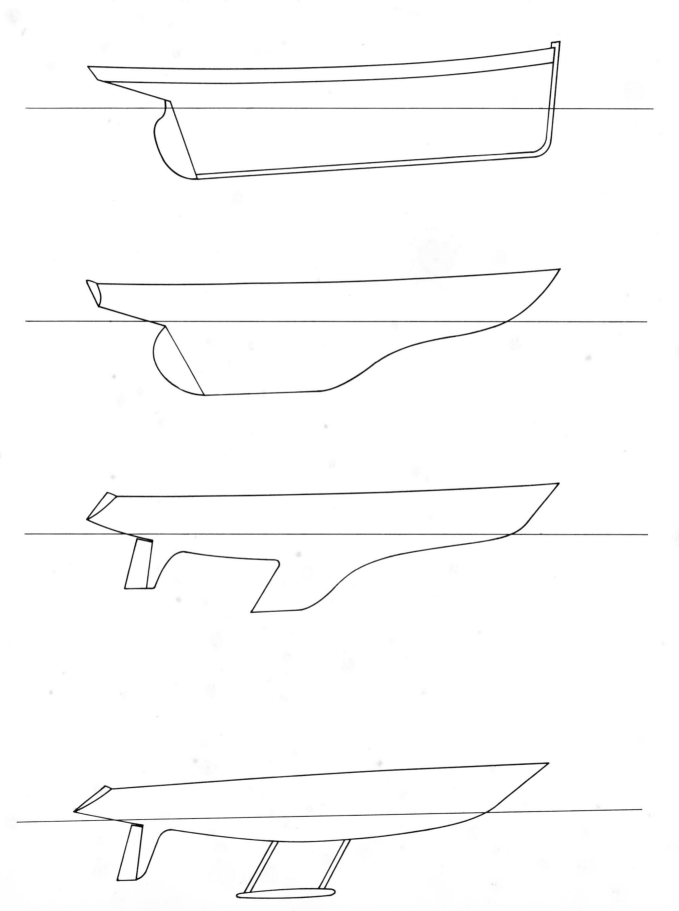

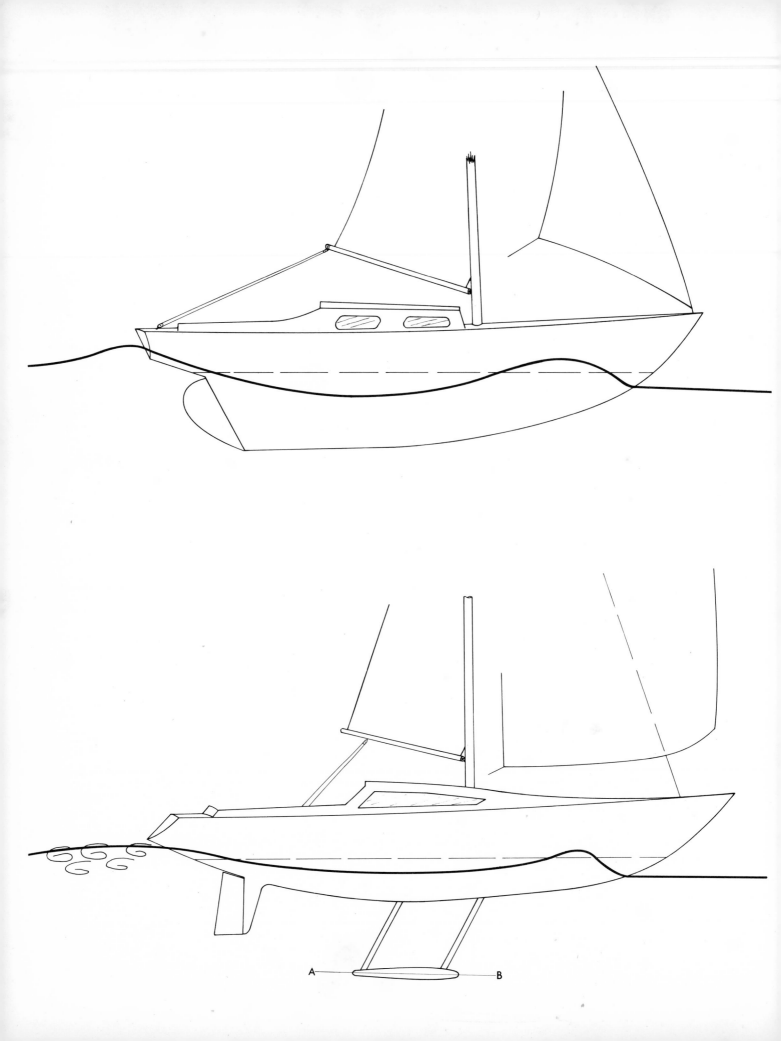

A ————————————————————— B

Fig. 2.4 (*left*). Wave form on different types of hull profile. Notice the accentuated wave form caused by the traditional displacement boat – the modern lifting keel type is approaching a planing condition having a flat wake.

Fig. 2.5. The drop-plate, fixed-ballast bulb racing yacht. The keel plate is arranged to slide up into the hull for off-wind sailing thereby reducing wetted surface and wave-making. The ballast bulb remains in position giving good sail-carrying capacity for all points of sailing.

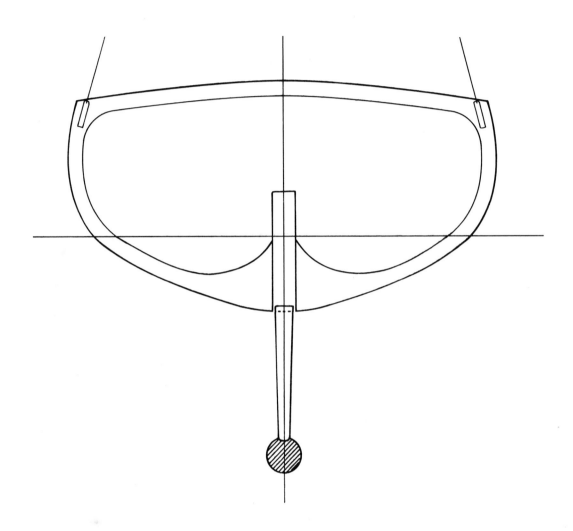

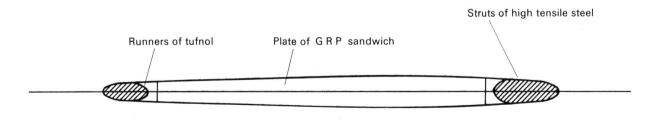

Struts of high tensile steel

Runners of tufnol

Plate of G R P sandwich

SECTION AT 'AA'

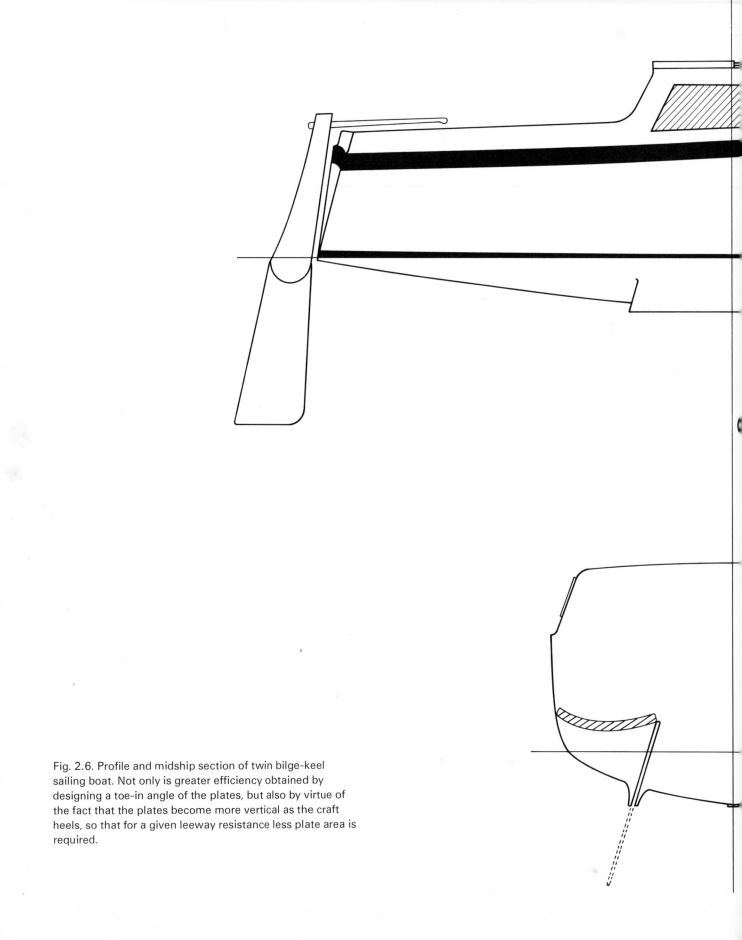

Fig. 2.6. Profile and midship section of twin bilge-keel
sailing boat. Not only is greater efficiency obtained by
designing a toe-in angle of the plates, but also by virtue of
the fact that the plates become more vertical as the craft
heels, so that for a given leeway resistance less plate area is
required.

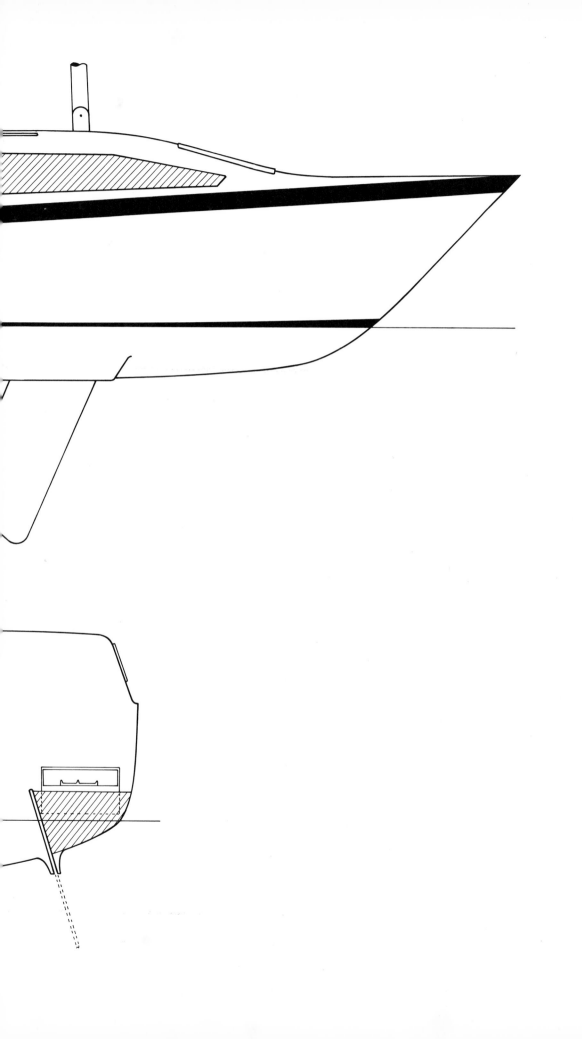

Plate 2 (*right*). *Myth of Malham* marks a milestone in the development of the modern offshore racer. Note the short overhangs and relatively high rig. The low-cut staysail fills the gap under the yankee jib, providing a low-pressure area on the back of the main at the foot. *Photo:* Beken

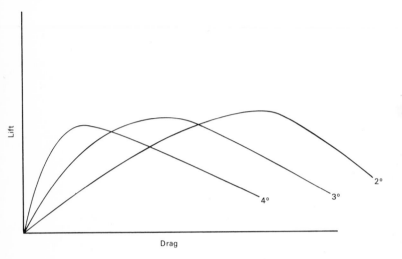

Fig. 2.7. Graph of lift/drag ratios at different angles of attack. These curves show the importance of choosing the correct toe-in angle bilge keels.

that the skin friction is higher than necessary due to the area of keel exposed to produce the lateral resistance. This effect is eliminated by using twin keels angled to the centreline, also giving a small angle of toe-in enabling some lift to be produced from the keel as well as a slight increase in lateral area when heeled. The drawings (Fig. 2.6) show plans of a boat using this feature. It is important that the toe-in angle should be carefully studied. The graph (Fig. 2.7) gives some idea of lift to drag ratios for various angles.

When going to starboard tack the port keel is lowered and the starboard keel may be raised, providing maximum leeway resistance for minimum wetted surface area. Hull stability is obtained by virtue of the beam of the vessel and by incorporating lead in the base of the drop keels.

One of the milestones in the development of the modern offshore racer was the conception of the yacht *Myth of Malham*. She was designed mainly as a racing machine when most other offshore racing yachts tended to be designed as good cruising sea boats, of high speed potential. She had a long waterline for her length overall, a small but high-aspect ratio mainsail situated fairly far aft, and was built to light scantlings. She proved her worth by winning her way through many offshore events through the 1947 and following seasons. This pointed the way to modern boat development. The modern offshore racing yacht has tended to be a very good performer off the wind due to light displacement and relatively low wetted area, so that it tends to surf or begin to plane under certain conditions. Performance to windward has slightly diminished due to wide beam and reduced stability. This has been demonstrated by the fact that the long-keel heavy displacement yachts can beat their lighter opponents if a race involves much windward work. Thus, offshore planing types, such as *Improbable* and *Windward Passage*, are unable to beat old heavy boats of finer form, such as the ex-12-Metre *American Eagle*. Designers will now be scratching their heads to try to get the best of both worlds, and methods of achieving this are discussed later in this chapter.

As mentioned earlier, one of the most important factors which has led to increase of speed in the modern offshore sailing yacht has been the adoption of a fin and skeg profile. This has the effect of decreasing both skin friction, as the wetted surface area is considerably reduced, and wave-making resistance, which is a function of waterline length and underwater hull form. However, it is important to get in perspective the relation of wave-making resistance to skin friction. A typical resistance curve for an offshore racing yacht is shown in Fig. 2.8. At a speed/length ratio of about 1 : 3 a single wave traverses the complete waterline of the yacht. If the

Fig. 2.9 (*right*). Comparison of wetted surfaces of two types. The long-keel slack-bilged boat has about 20 per cent less wetted surface than the canoe-bodied fin and skeg type.

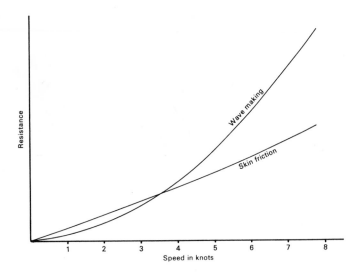

Fig. 2.8. Wave-making and skin resistance curves for a typical 40-ft offshore racer. Note that in light weather skin friction is the important factor.

yacht is not able to lift and plane, the wave-making resistance curve continues to increase rapidly. The skin friction will continue to increase, but at a lesser rate. It can be seen from the Figure that for a typical fin and skeg hull form with a clean bottom it is only at very low speeds that the wave-making and skin-friction resistances are similar in magnitude. The diagrams of wave forms (Fig. 2.4) show that for the long-keel yacht the wave troughs and crests are much larger than for the shallow hull form for equal speed/length ratios. The depth of this wave is proportional to the square of the resistance. The reader may see from this simplified explanation why, if high speed is of prime consideration, the change to shallow hulls with fin and skeg has evolved.

This does not mean that the fin and skeg configuration is best in all conditions. In very light winds a slack-bilge, long-keeled yacht is sometimes faster than its shallow-fin counterpart, as the wetted

Fig. 2.9 (*right*). Comparison of wetted surfaces of two types. The long-keel slack-bilged boat has about 20 per cent less wetted surface than the canoe-bodied fin and skeg type.

surface area may be greater for the latter. Fig. 2.9 shows two yacht hull types with their associated wetted surface area where the slack-bilge, long-keel type is marginally faster under very light winds, that is, a $V/\sqrt{L}$ of less than 0·2 for a yacht of 36-ft waterline, corresponding to a speed of 1·4 knots, requiring a wind speed of 2 to 3 knots.

What does all this indicate in predicting future trends for yacht hull design? There will always be a case for the long-keel hull form if shallow draft is required, on the grounds that to get sufficient leeway resistance without a deep keel, the keel should extend along the underwater hull form as far as possible. Modern sailing yachts with the area of keel concentrated around midships require considerably more draught for their sail-carrying capacity than did their last-century predecessors, which achieved most of the resistance to leeway by flat areas of hull form at the ends of the vessel (Fig. 2.10). The long-keel type has the added advantage that it is steadier on the helm, particularly in downwind conditions, avoiding the more frequent broaching exhibited by the fin and skeg types.

As far as ultimate speed is concerned, ignoring effects of the rating rules, the underwater hull form will continue to be cut away with a deepening in the keel to get maximum efficiency from it. The rudder will be moved as far aft as is practicable and, for larger yachts of say 64-ft waterline and over, a more balanced underwater curve of areas will be adopted. Smaller yachts will tend to have a less balanced curve of areas because their planing or surfing ability is increased by flattening out the hull form aft, but although this shape will not be quite as fast as the balanced form under lighter wind conditions, they have potentially higher maximum speeds. It will be realised from these comments that any particular hull form will be of optimum shape at one speed only. This is one of the reasons why yacht design is

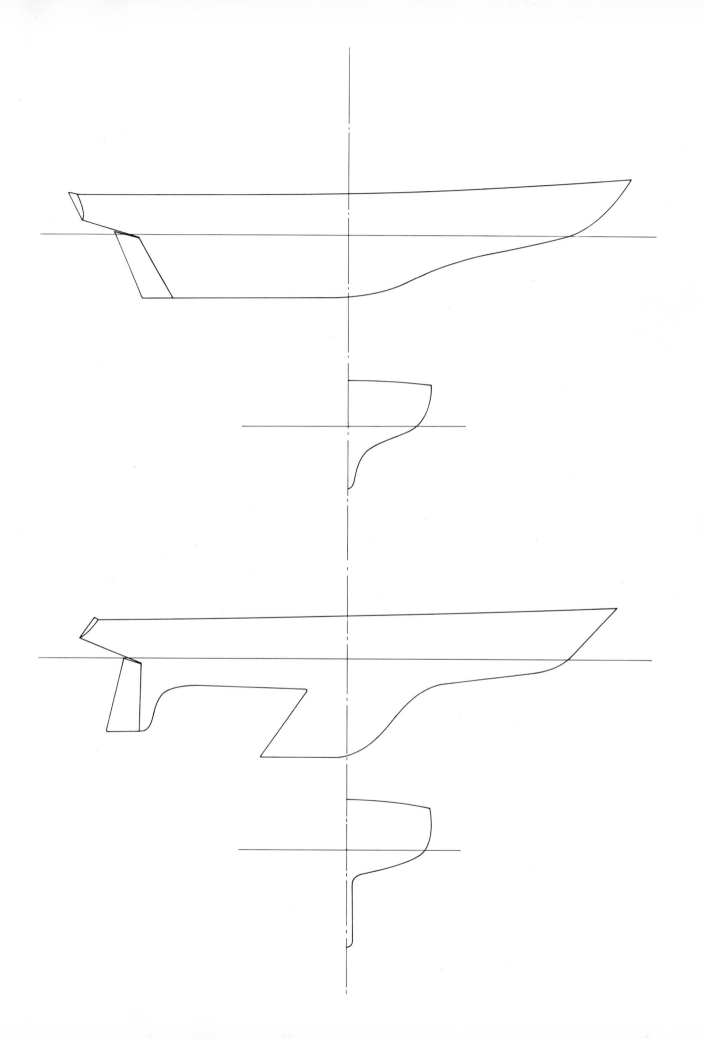

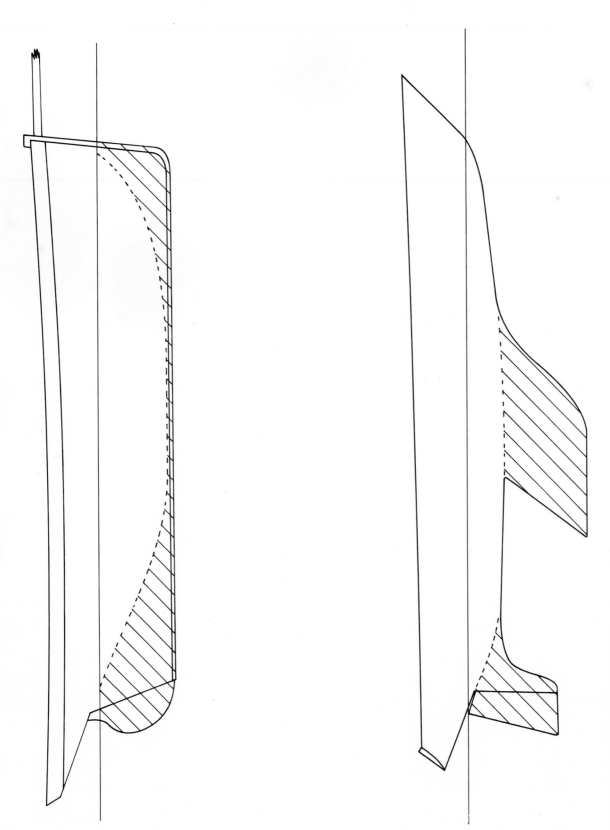

Fig. 2.10. Keel area distribution for early and modern types. The keel action on the old smack yacht is mainly derived from the ends, whereas the modern yacht derives lift from a short fin amidships and a skeg and rudder aft.

such a fascinating subject to the sailing enthusiast and naval architect, for in contrast perhaps to ship design, a 'correct' yacht hull does not exist.

Ways have been introduced to design hulls closer to the optimum under varying conditions by altering the underwater hull form. The most obvious example of this is the introduction of the drop keel. This is particularly advantageous in off-the-wind work where skin friction may be considerably reduced, as large resistance to leeway is not required. There are circumstances where the keel area can be reduced with advantage when going to windward, for there is a critical heeling angle, usually between 30° and 40°, above which the yacht starts to slow down (Fig. 2.11). Thus, under gusty conditions, sail can be reduced or the keel can be raised to reduce lateral resistance, thereby decreasing heel. With this reduction in keel area leeway need not necessarily increase because the hull form becomes more efficient and the speed of the yacht will be improved, due not only to the reduction in heel but also to the reduction in wetted surface area. A second more extreme way of altering underwater shape to give a performance near optimum at different values of $V/\sqrt{L}$ would be to alter the hull form itself. It might be possible to bolt on different sections at the bow and stern according to expected wind conditions. This may sound a little fantastic, but the amount of money and thought now put into achieving marginally better speeds by altering rig and sails could be more than equalled in effectiveness by altering the dimensions of the yacht. This would undoubtedly cause a headache for the rule measurers! One can imagine this idea being applicable particularly to, say, Quarter Ton Cup boats, built of aluminium alloy or GRP.

Offshore racing has increased in popularity quite dramatically over the past fifteen years, though it is still true to say that it is undertaken by only a small

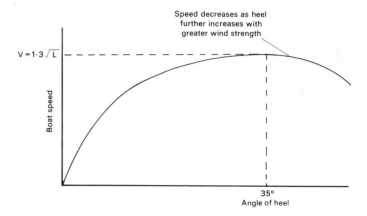

Fig. 2.11. A graph showing speed at different angles of heel. If the heel angle increases beyond about 30°–40° speed will be lost.

fraction of those sailing. Many of the races sailed by these offshore racers are not of the true offshore type such as the Bermuda, Fastnet and Sidney–Hobart. A Class I offshore racing yacht today costs anything from £40,000 upwards, so there is a strong case for a well-built and fast one-design class, particularly as rule changes (unless the owner goes to the large expense of having the underwater form altered) tend to make many of the latest-designed racers noncompetitive within two or three years. Yachts competing in the classes of the Offshore Rule tend to be designed around the rule, but this does not mean to say that they are fast craft. As far as aesthetics are concerned many of the latest designs, particularly for Quarter and Half Ton Cup classes, are very unattractive. There is little justification in designing a floating monstrosity purely to gain maximum advantage out of an artificial rule. This does not further the science of designing intrinsically fast craft. Aesthetically speaking most would agree that the beautiful lines of the 30 Square Metre will always be admired and that the fat offshore racer with short overhangs and lack of sheer does not compare.

Day boats and one-designs of any kind can score heavily in hours under way per annum, compared with cruiser-racers which usually sail in far more concentrated and expensive doses, often not too much enjoyed by the owner's family which has to choose between staying at home or facing a sick-making voyage.

There are other considerations too. Inshore racing allows yachtsmen to work from a weekend house in a yachting port, giving them better accommodation and the ability to entertain in comfort. The pleasures of racing and sailing in local waters, even in yachts which are large cruising auxiliaries conforming to the Offshore Rule, make a strong case for more international one-design day boats and offshore racers. Day boats are sailed from all the world's large sailing centres such as Cowes, Marblehead, Sydney, Cannes and Capetown. A two- to six-hour race in a hot class of keelboat, big enough not to need acrobatics and able to cleave a way through wind-over-tide chop in long windward slices, gives satisfaction at a much reduced financial outlay.

The 11-Metre (Figs. 2.12 and 2.13) is a day-racing boat designed to meet the need for a displacement craft of this type. Her length of 36 ft and fine beam enable her to go to windward faster than most comparable craft of equivalent waterline. It is necessary for a yacht of this type to adopt a length of this order, even though she becomes less manageable on a trailer than the present smaller day-racing keelboat, to perform as a proper keelboat under extreme sea and wind conditions. It is important, also, to ensure that the displacement is such that the crew need not hang along the deck edge or sit out, as in dinghy racing, to make the boat go well to windward. The *Dragon* has possibly the smallest length that could be adopted to fulfil these requirements, but she is far heavier than need be for her length due to her form of construction. The long ends may be criticised by some, but the whole aim of the design has been to combine excellent windward

performance with an aesthetically pleasing profile. The keel configuration of the Eleven conforms to latest design theory and incorporates a trim tab operated by a worm control gear. As will be mentioned in Chapter 7, it is important to design a craft carefully for the material of which she is built. The design shown is prepared solely for GRP construction with great attention to ensure ease of moulding. However, in order to obtain minimum displacement the laminating should be carried out to a high technical standard which can only be achieved by the skill of craftsmen laminators.

The ballast is fitted inside the hull shell. It is true that this does not give the highest possible ballast ratio due to the thickness of GRP covering the ballast keel, but it avoids the curse of leaking keelbolts and subsequent damage to the GRP so common in some yachts of the fin and skeg type having a very narrow top face to the keel. The pressure to reduce weight in order to win races with boats of lighter displacement is notable in the work of many offshore racing yacht designers. However, at the cost of a small reduction in speed a yacht may be constructed far more soundly, thus doing away with the necessity for continual repairs and offering a longer life expectancy.

The clean, streamlined deck layout in the Eleven is achieved by integral moulding of many deck fittings, hatches and recesses. The sliding foredeck hatch recess is drained to the waterline preventing water accumulation in the channel. The 290-sq ft mainsail is fully battened for improved camber control with double luff running in twin mast tracks (Chapter 5). Reefing is by lacing through eyelets across the sail engaging with hooks along the boom giving quick simple reefing with even tension along the sail, thus permitting the kicking strap to remain in place. The overlap of the large foresail is less extreme than that encouraged by current rating rules

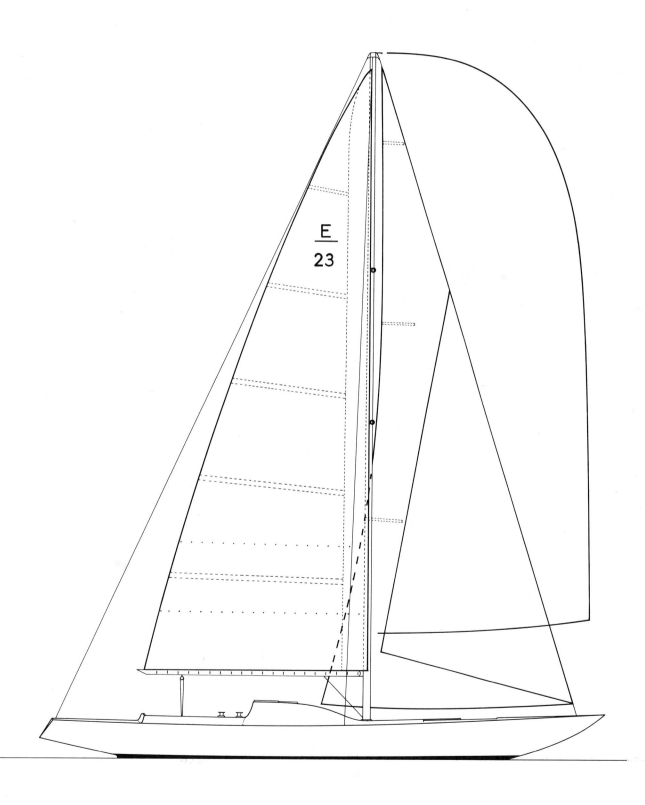

Fig. 2.13. General arrangements and deck plan of the 11th Metre. The boat is designed for GRP construction with very special attention given to the stiffening in the forward end.

but is closer to the optimum performance proportions. The shrouds and halyards all lead through deck fittings with the tensions transmitted to the heel of the mast enabling a triangle of forces to be set up, to remove the strain of shrouds from the topsides.

The minimum racing crew is three, but provision is made for a fourth. The helmsman sits in the aft end of the large cockpit, which is flanked by foresail and spinnaker sheet winches on a coaming carried well out to the side giving the helmsman a better view from leeward when heeled. The main sheet runs on a track on a low bridge deck at the forward end of the helm area, the falls leading to a winch mounted horizontally on the bulkhead. The cockpit is watertight and has a radiused bottom and curved helmsman's seat.

The interior arrangements are geared to day sailing but are both flexible and well designed so that even the most committed 12-Metre enthusiast will be attracted to this sleek but inexpensive racer.

One of the most interesting trials of recent years was the 1972 World Sailing Speed Record at Weymouth, England. The course for the race was laid out in a circle so that the competitors could sail at maximum speed along a diameter of the circle in any direction. Many unusual craft entered, with most design enthusiasm concentrated on sailing hydrofoils. The winner *Crossbow* clocked 26·3 knots in a 19-knot wind (a speed/wind ratio of 1:4), but could sail at twice the wind speed for lower wind strengths; she is a proa with the outrigger to windward. Stability is achieved by the crew running up a catwalk to the outrigger as the vessel heels. The 60-ft main hull is constructed of cold-moulded wood and she sets nearly 1000 sq ft of sail. She is designed to sail on one tack only in order to get the utmost from the rig and deck layout. The next boat was a

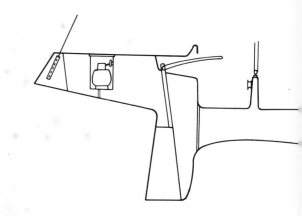

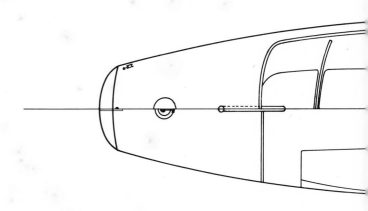

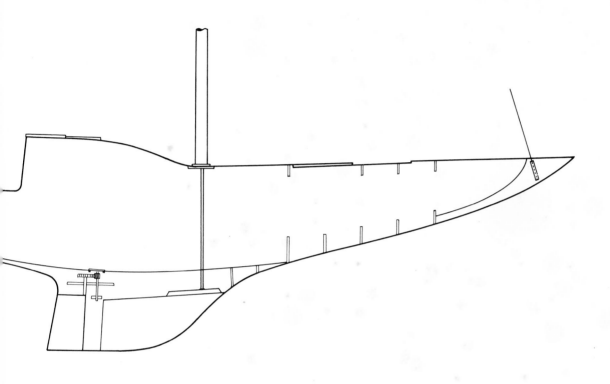

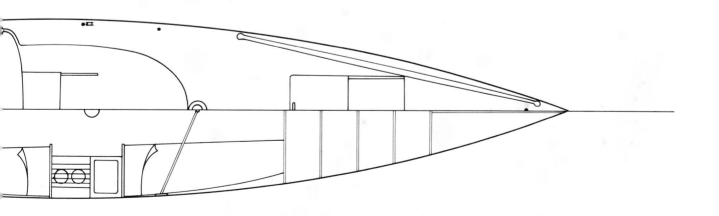

Fig. 2.14. Length/displacement curve for typical offshore racers. The crew weight curve demonstrates the importance of correct positioning of crew in smaller craft.

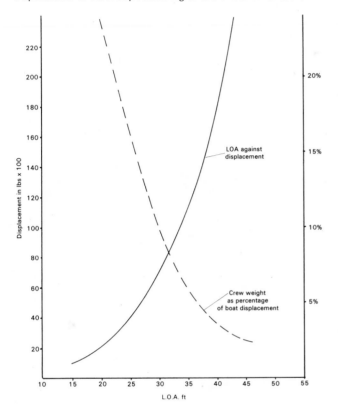

percentage of displacement. For the small yacht it is important to keep the crew in the best possible position, that is as far out to windward as can be comfortably achieved. Fig. 2.15 shows an interesting design enabling wetted surface area to be cut to a minimum for light weather work. The bulges on the sides of the hull give a great increase in stability as the yacht heels to 25°, and inside, act as a shelf on which bunks can be sited. The deck area is very wide for the length, giving ease in handling sail and also allowing a wide track to be fitted under the boom halfway along its length. This acts as a mainsheet traveller and holds the boom well down well off the wind, eliminating twist from the mainsail. A wide slot can be achieved for the genoa for light windward work or sailing off the wind. This type of craft would be difficult and expensive to build in timber, but in GRP would be relatively easy.

The trend over the last few years has been towards the light-displacement ocean racer which has achieved most of the racing successes. There have been one or two exceptions such as *American Eagle* and *Ticonderoga*, but these heavier-displacement craft tend to do well only in heavy weather or if there is a lot of windward work. Hull scantlings have become as light as can be accepted using conventional materials and construction, provided the yacht is to be in reasonable condition after five years' hard racing, so more attention is being given to saving non-structural weight. Chapter 8 points out methods for saving weight but it is enough, here, to say that with careful attention the displacement of a typical 40-ft racing yacht may be reduced by 900 lb, or 6 per cent.

Strangely enough the overall weight of deck fittings has increased in the modern offshore racing yacht as the number of winches and their size has greatly increased. Class I offshore racers are now using 'coffee grinders' which not only increase

sailing hydrofoil but this proved to be nearly 5 knots slower. The series will undoubtedly assist development in multihull design and encourage sailing hydrofoils. *Crossbow* was much longer than the runners-up, indicating that length is still a major factor where ultimate speed is of prime consideration.

As the displacement of offshore racers decreases, crew weight becomes an important feature. Classes such as Quarter Tonners are tending to become overgrown dinghies. The graph (Fig. 2.14) shows the overall length against displacement for a typical offshore racing yacht, and also the crew weight as a

Fig. 2.15. Section through bulge-sided yacht. Notice the great increase in waterline beam when heeled to 25°. This type of hull has a very low wetted surface when sailed upright.

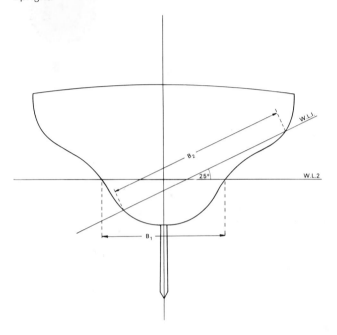

weight well above the keel if mounted on deck but also require additional deck structure and represent detrimental windage. If it is necessary to adopt such fittings, then it is important that they should be mounted as low as possible. Since the winch man should see what is going on, there is much to be said for the introduction of larger cockpit areas, similar to the arrangements on the modern 12-Metres, if he is below normal deck level. These could be fitted with sliding hatches incorporating rubber gaskets for wet work. Heavy items such as the chain cable would be stowed above the keel by leading the chain through a plastic pipe to a capstan mounted below the cabin sole; the chain would then fall into a bin on the ballast keel. In an emergency a brake would be released allowing the chain to run out freely.
It would be preferable still to have the anchor stowed on deck forward or up in the stem in case of emergency, although the very keen racing

owners might well prefer to stow it above the ballast keel.

Keel shape is one of the most important features in the design of the fast offshore sailing yacht. Until quite recently argument raged among designers regarding the best keel cross-section and sharp versus blunt leading edges. Experienced helmsmen know how differently yachts will handle according to the section of the leading edge of the keel. Unfortunately, like many aspects of yacht design, the answer is not a clear right or wrong but varies according to speed and sea state. Research into this problem has indicated overall trends enabling the designer to design the keel with some degree of confidence for the expected conditions.

Fig. 2.16 shows the types of flow pattern that exist around a keel for varying leading edges and speeds. It will be observed that a sharp edge tends to induce much turbulence on the low pressure side, increasing the hull resistance. This will have a dramatic effect on the balance of the yacht, leading to confusion regarding the type of section to be adopted. Many times, similar yachts have been built, one with a sharp leading edge, the other blunt, with the former proving to be faster! This has arisen because the rig tended to be more balanced for the particular mast position on the yacht having the sharp-edged keel. Generally speaking, a sharp leading edge to the keel holds a yacht on a steadier course with increased weather helm. If the keel area in a fin-keel yacht is too small and the leading edge is rounded, then, when the yacht heels, her bow will tend to fall off the wind. It could be said that a sharp keel gives some grip on the water, with some increase of resistance for the speeds normally encountered in sailing.

The trailing edge of the keel should also be given special attention. Although the Offshore Rule does not, encourage the use of trim tabs, they are

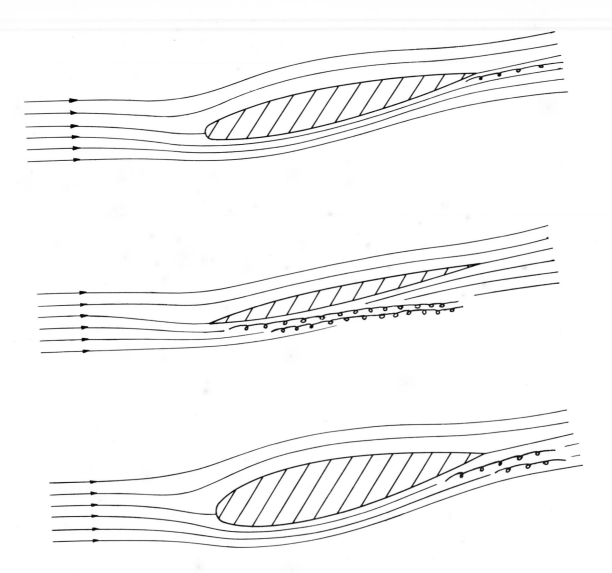

undoubtedly beneficial to performance. They are angled up to windward to give hydrodynamic lift from the keel surface, in the same way that aircraft flaps are partially lowered on takeoff to give maximum aerodynamic lift. This results in a considerable reduction in leeway and, provided the yacht is balanced and the trim tab is set to the correct angle (which should be approximately 4° at 5 knots), the helmsman feels as if the yacht is creeping up bodily to windward. For lift at slow speeds the angle of attack should be increased, but with caution, for a stalling effect can easily be created. Ideally the whole keel should be angled to give the required lift, but in fixed-keel boats this is structurally very difficult. To overcome this difficulty tabs at both the leading and trailing edges could be fitted with a relatively narrow section of fixed keel between; this would produce a similar effect to angling the keel as a whole. The tabs could be operated by a worm gear, which should be turned on tacking to reverse the angle of attack.

Multihulls and Proas

Before closing this chapter, mention should be made of multihulls; craft which deserve more publicity and encouragement and should not be disregarded by cruising and racing men. The sailing of multihulled boats has increased steadily in popularity since the middle of the nineteenth century. There is no reason for their popularity to decline in the future but they do pose particular

Fig. 2.16 (*left*). Flow pattern from leading edge of different keel types. It can be seen that keels with a sharp leading edge and keels of high thickness : chord ratio cause turbulence.

Fig. 2.17. An early Herreshoff catamaran – the *John Gilpin*. Note that the curved beams joining the hulls are connected with universal joints to reduce stress.

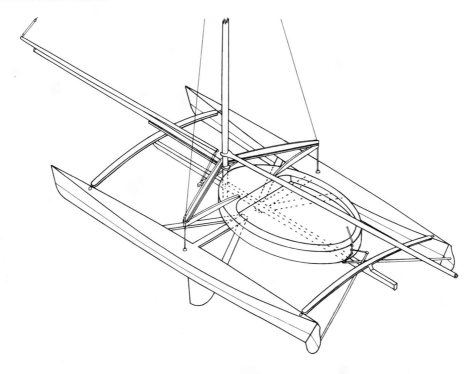

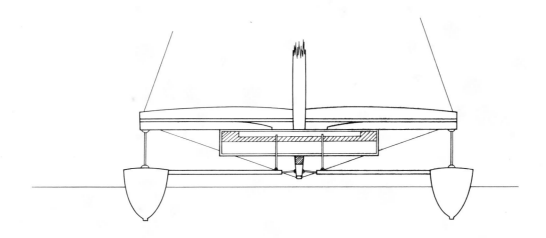

problems for designers and yachtsmen which will influence their future.

N. G. Herreshoff introduced a catamaran in America in 1876. He described it as being slow in stays and inclined to pitchpole or upset longitudinally. The hulls of these early boats also had a tendency to work at the joint with the bridge deck, and sometimes to wrench away in rough conditions; a tendency which is still observable in multihulls today. Herreshoff attempted to overcome the latter problem when designing *Amarylls*, *Aryan*, *Teaser*, *Tarantella* and *John Gilpin*, by joining the hulls with trussed curved beams, connected by universal joints to ease the high stresses imposed at these points (Fig. 2.17).

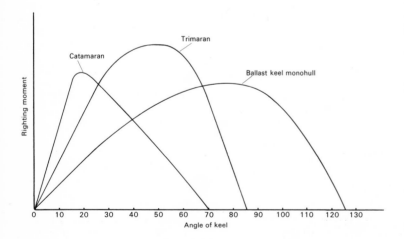

Fig. 2.18. Stability curves for catamarans and trimarans and monohulls. Notice that although the initial stability of the multihulls is better than that of the monohull, the angles of vanishing stability are less satisfactory.

Despite modifications in design, catamarans are regarded with suspicion and caution by yachtsmen for they are capsizable. The keel boat relies on ballast for stability so that, as the angle of heel increases up to 90°, the righting moment increases. The catamaran, however, starts to lose its intrinsic stability as the heel reaches 20° (Fig. 2.18). And in gale conditions, if the weather hull leaves the surface, the wind can catch under a solid bridge deck and capsize the craft.

The instability of the catamaran is, therefore, inherent in its basic design. However, modifications can be made to ensure that when a capsize takes place it can be dealt with in the most efficient manner. Thus the mast of a catamaran should have a float at the top or it should be of sufficient buoyancy to prevent its turning right over. A system using a laterally-hinged rotating wing mast (Fig. 2.19) would be particularly helpful. This idea incorporates one heavy continuous shroud attached via pulleys at the ends of the cross-beam members to a powered winch on the bridging deck. In the event of capsize, either to port or starboard, a brake on the winch is released and the shroud is shortened on the side lying on the water while automatically increasing the length of the opposite shroud. It should be noted that only two shrouds are required in this rig as the least radius of gyration of the wing mast is more than enough to provide adequate lateral stability. When the catamaran is winched into the horizontal position employing the great buoyancy of the mast, the winch is reversed to hoist the mast while feathered to the wind direction. In the case of large catamarans, the winch could be electrically driven by dry cells for the capsize emergency, with an automatic trigger device which operates when the rig is inclined at 90° to the vertical.

Trimarans do not suffer so much from the capsizing disadvantage since they combine the

Fig. 2.19. Rotating mast for righting multihulls. A winch on the bridge deck is used to haul in the appropriate shroud.

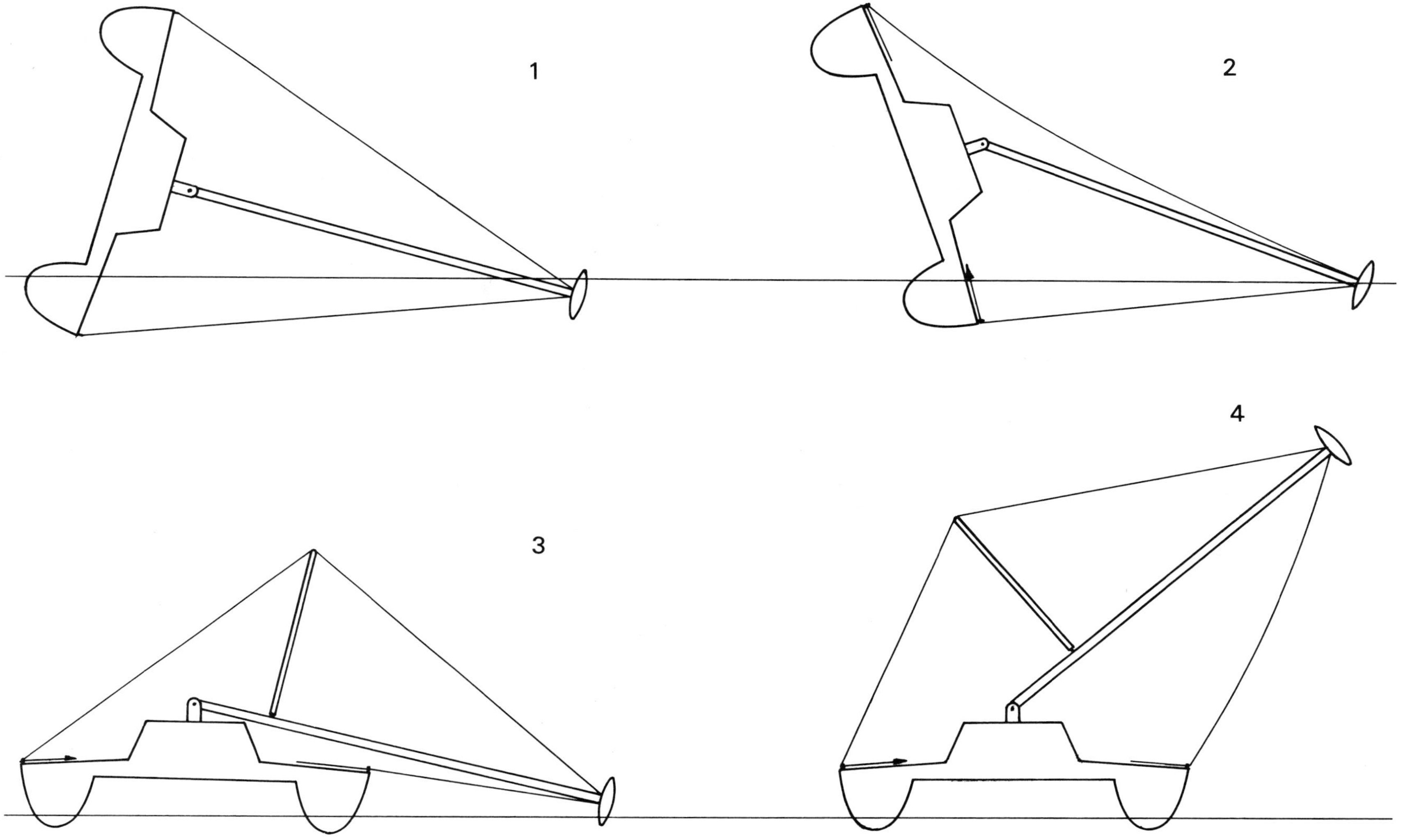

Plate 3 (*left*). *Pen Duick IV*, now named *Manureva*, is one of the fastest sailing craft afloat. Recent modifications have given her bows more flare and buoyancy to prevent nose-diving at speed. *Photo:* Beken

Fig. 2.20. Tacking principle for proas. The boat is brought to a halt when going about and the rig has to be swapped end for end.

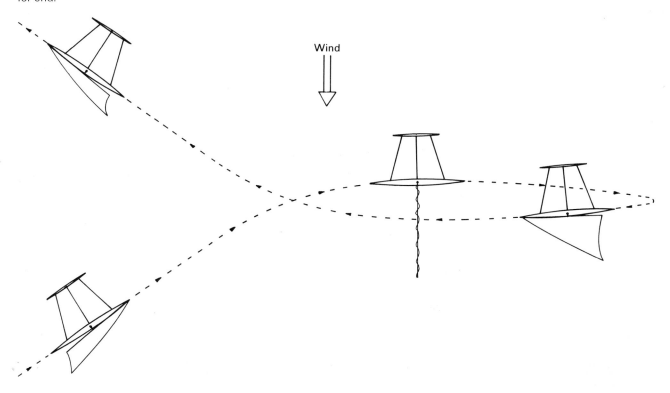

Wind

stability of the catamaran's beam with the ballasted stability of the monohull. It is expected, therefore, that the popularity of trimarans will increase more quickly than that of catamarans.

The safety aspect apart, multihulls compare quite favourably with monohulls in performance. For example, in strong winds where the keel boat monohull soon reaches a speed/length ratio to the value of 1:4, and wave-making resistance soars, the light displacement of the catamaran and to a lesser extent of the trimaran – both relying on beam for stability – means that the multihulls will lift in the water to assume a semi-planing condition as they have far less wave-making resistance.

Multihulls are slower in very light winds, particularly to windward, as a result of their large surface area. Nevertheless, a high performance can be expected as was demonstrated by Tabarly's *Pen Duick IV* when she set up the record from Los Angeles to Honolulu, and when she crossed the Atlantic in 11 days at an average of 280 miles per day. The ultimate speed of the trimaran is not as great as that of the catamaran but, as long as the central hull is not excessive in breadth/length ratio, good speeds can be achieved. As far as handling is concerned, the trimaran is designed to have less float buoyancy than that of the catamaran and the crew can easily see when it is being pressed too hard as the leeward hull is forced under water. To reduce wetted surface area the outriggers of the trimaran should be designed so that the windward rigger will not be in contact with the surface. In port, it is

Plate 4. *Cheers*, a proa designed for long-distance single-handed sailing. She proved to be completely balanced, requiring no self-steering gear. Note the fully rotating rig and double-ended hulls for tacking. *Photo:* Beken

Plate 5 (*right*). *Toria*, now *Gancia Girl*, at great speed on a fine reach. Note the large twist in the reefed main, resulting in poor sail efficiency over the full luff length. The jib halyard needs tightening. *Photo:* Beken

Fig. 2.21. Roller cross beam principle for a proa. This system permits the craft to tack conventionally, thus eliminating the necessity for rotating rig and permitting much greater tacking efficiency.

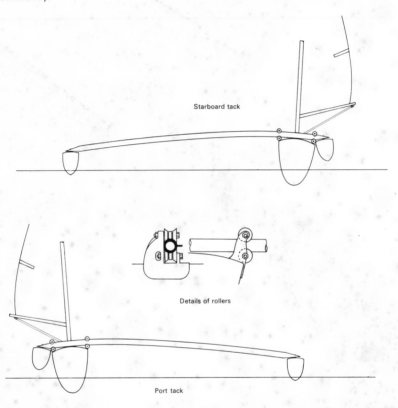

Starboard tack

Details of rollers

Port tack

necessary to ballast the craft to lie on only one outrigger so that it does not flop from one keel to the other. Thus, with careful design and sensible handling, the poor windward performance of the multihull compared with the modern monohull in light winds is compensated for by its high speed potential and comfort in strong beam or following winds, ensuring that the multihull will play a prominent part in the development of sailing yachts in the future.

One further sailing yacht type that should be discussed is the proa. The proa has gained favour during recent years particularly following the fine performance of the 40-ft *Cheers*, which achieved a close third behind *Sir Thomas Lipton* and *Voortrekker* in the 1968 Singlehanded Transatlantic Race. In beating the larger multihulls *Cheers* managed to record the best day's run when she sailed 225 nautical miles. She was so well balanced that she did not require self-steering gear, partly because this type of craft swings its rig about to sail on the other tack in order that the outrigger is always to leeward (or to windward in some types) (Fig. 2.20). There are interesting developments in the design of the proa, the most notable of which is the adoption of a system of rollers on the main hull allowing a beam, supporting outriggers at each end, to run between the rollers when tacking (Fig. 2.21). This arrangement greatly assists the proa in going to windward in short tacks as, otherwise, considerable distance is lost each time the craft goes about.

3

The motor yacht

The Background

Compared with sailing yachts, power craft have a very recent though complex history of development. Speed under power afloat was first achieved with steam-driven craft. The early steam yachts of the mid-nineteenth century were often fairly fast, speeds of up to 14 knots being attained, but it was in steam launches, day boats up to 70 ft, that the development of high speed was achieved. Much of this early development was carried out in Britain, with firms such as John I. Thornycroft taking a leading part, closely paralleled in America by yards such as the Herreshoff Manufacturing Company. While most of the British fast steam craft were being built as torpedo boats or other government types, the pattern of American yachting and of the business life of the power-yacht enthusiast resulted in the development of small fast steamers to cover as great a distance in as short a time as possible in order to make most use of limited leisure. This in turn inspired the development of the express cruiser in America almost a century ago, and a few firms brought the construction of these craft to a high state of perfection using reciprocating engines of very advanced design. This was rivalled in Britain where steam torpedo boats and destroyers were achieving speeds up to 31·5 knots in 1898.

A year previously, the fast steam launch *Turbinia*, designed and built by the Parsons Engineering Company especially to demonstrate the power, reliability and compactness of the steam turbine, had shown her paces at the Spithead Naval Review, where the spectacle of a sleek hundred-footer dashing through the fleet had attracted the attention intended. Before long many destroyers and steam yachts were fitted with steam turbines and were followed soon after by battleships and the largest liners. However, turbines were not developed for very small craft, so small steam yachts and launches continued with reciprocating engines until they were ousted by internal combustion machinery.

Petrol and diesel engines were being fitted in pleasure craft in the late 1890s, and were readily accepted as a progressive means of propulsion in America, where by about 1907 petrol-engine motor boats were common among pleasure and commercial craft and also as auxiliary motors in sailing craft. In Britain, early petrol-engined pleasure craft followed two main types: yacht launches and a seaworthy type of motor cruiser usually between 35 and 50 ft long and often carrying auxiliary sails. Shortly before the First World War some substantial motor yachts having diesel machinery were being built in Britain and America.

During this period racing in both countries had developed some extremely fast motor boats, many of them having stepped bottoms (Fig. 3.1) and often being driven by complex petrol engines designed by the hull designer (such as Clinton Crane, William Atkin etc.), a trend particularly noticeable in America.

The accelerated development of petrol marine engines during the First World War enabled extremely fast small warships to be built not only in Britain and America but with marked success in Italy and Russia, both of whose navies had large numbers of these useful torpedo, anti-submarine and patrol craft. In Britain the design and development of the motor torpedo boat was largely undertaken by John I. Thornycroft & Co, whose stepped-bottom boats were capable of up to 55 knots in war trim; a remarkable achievement considering the engine weight per horsepower produced. Post-war development of diesel engines enabled power yachts of a larger size to be built and, until the Depression years of the late 1920s, their numbers increased steadily in America, although many British owners

Fig. 3.1. Profile of an early stepped hull motor boat.
Stepped hulls gave superb speed/displacement figures but
steadily lost favour because of structural problems.

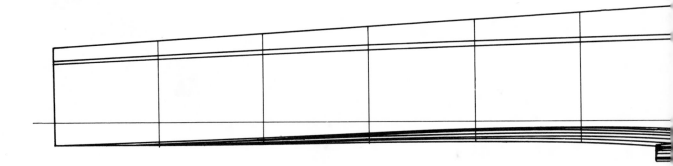

Plate 6. *Oma*, 1920, a high-speed experimental craft using
an aircraft engine. These early fast craft tended to be very
wet in any seaway. *Photo:* Beken

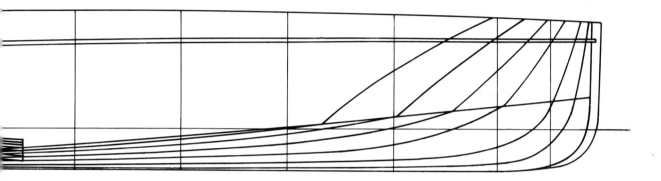

still favoured steam. The trend towards diesel motor yachts strengthened in Britain throughout the 1930s and became general thereafter.

In contrast to these large yachts, the 1920s saw the rapid development of small series-produced petrol-engined motor cruisers aimed at the middle-class market. The exhilaration of wartime experiences in fast naval craft led a few enthusiasts to order similar boats as yachts. The express cruiser of those inter-war years, pioneered by Hubert Scott-Payne, is the direct ancestor of the present deep-V 30-knot motor yacht. Specialised motor-boat racing lagged in Britain after 1914 until it was revived in the 1960s, but development of extreme high-speed planing craft was maintained for attempts at water-speed records.

In Germany during the late 1920s a reconstituted naval fleet encouraged the design and development of motor torpedo boats of a type having in common with the steam torpedo boats of a quarter century before, their length to breadth proportion of 6 to 1. Their hulls were of round-bilge form, capable of high sustained speed at sea. More important still, the Germans foresaw the crucial development of the high-speed, low-weight, compact marine diesel

engine, and this foresight had provided by 1939 an efficient force of *Schnellboot*, colloquially known in Britain as E-boats.

In Britain firms were pioneering a different form of torpedo boat, having single-chine hulls capable of speeds up to 40 knots under favourable conditions, being powered with foreign-made petrol engines such as the Isotta Fraschini, Hall Scott, Packard and Stirling, which were not so reliable at sea as diesels. Thus the principal differences of the opposing light fleets continued until the end of hostilities, during which time the US Navy adopted and developed the British pattern of motor torpedo boats (MTBs), renamed PT boats. Due to the weight of wartime equipment and armament the range and speed of these craft did not exceed, or even in many cases approach, that of the earlier types.

The design of motor yachts after the war followed no set pattern. Most were under 50 ft, though size increased during the 1960s, reaching a climax in craft of over 300 ft. Hulls were of accepted round-bilge or single-chine form until the racing success of the deep-V form principally developed by the American designer Raymond Hunt.

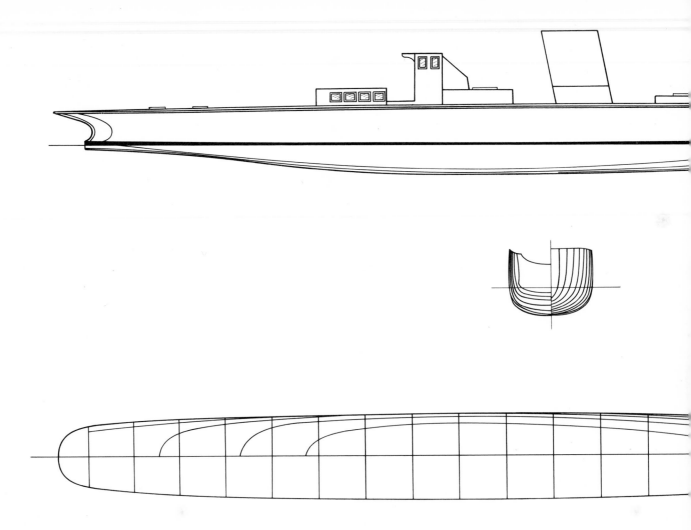

In order to predict hull forms for the future, it is necessary to distinguish between the motor yacht and the cruising type and high-speed racing yacht.

The most interesting development is that of racing types, as these tend to show the way for cruising-yacht trends. Although many of the Class I power boats today look very extreme in form and leave little room for accommodation, the present deep-V hull shape incorporating spray rails and having a long pointed bow has evolved through the necessity for a hull form capable of maintaining high speeds in a seaway. The early high-speed craft tended to have a long narrow form and were almost exclusively round-bilged.

The *Turbinia*, mentioned earlier, was built in 1897, attaining a speed of 35 knots with steam turbines delivering 2000 h.p. at 2000 r.p.m. She displaced 44·5 tons on a waterline length of 100 ft (Fig. 3.2). The designer, Sir Charles Parsons, took as a basis for the lines for this craft the rowing eight, as it was known at that time that these long narrow boats required the least power to drive them at their speed of approximately 9 knots.

This round hull form tended to be used up to just before the First World War, when experiments were carried out with flat-bottomed chine boats, as it was discovered that they required less power to achieve a planing condition than the round-bilged hulls. It was proved that hydrostatic lift is proportional to the angle of attack and area of planing surface, for a plate trimmed about an axis in line with the water surface (Fig. 3.3). Thus, to develop a fast-planing hull the requirement is a wide, flat bottom aft, provided an accurate longitudinal centre of gravity and centre of pressure can be determined to achieve the required trim. Such a hull form has a great disadvantage, however, in that it is subjected to severe pounding when travelling in any sort of

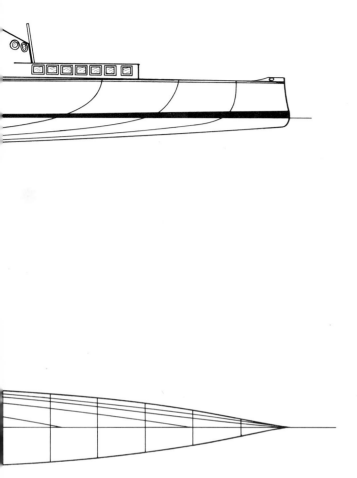

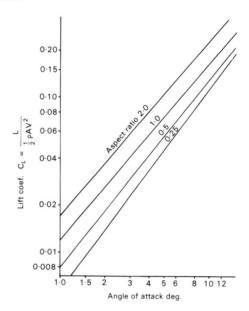

Fig. 3.2 (*left*). *Turbinia*'s profile, sections and plan. The hull of this 35-knot craft was based on the lines of rowing eights.

Fig. 3.3 (*below*). Graph of lift against angle of attack for a planing plate. Note that with increasing breadth : length ratio (aspect ratio) the lift increases but of course the susceptibility to pounding in a seaway at speed also increases.

seaway. Thus it was discovered that the design of the planing motor yacht is an awkward compromise between hydrostatic lift and sea-keeping quality.

Throughout the last seventy years many interesting solutions to this problem have been advanced. In 1912 *Mapleleaf IV* was designed and built by S. E. Saunders. With a waterline length of 40 ft she was the first boat to attain a speed of 50 knots, faster than many power boats racing today. She displaced $5\frac{1}{4}$ tons on petrol engines delivering 800 h.p. Fig. 3.4 shows *Mapleleaf IV* in section and profile, and it may be observed that she incorporates five steps in the hull form aft. Saunders had developed the stepped hull form from his earlier designs, as he found that it required far less power due to the effect of good hydrodynamic lift from an accurately determined angle of attack at each step. The hull bottom could be considered as equivalent to a succession of planing plates (Fig. 3.3). Following

the great success of this craft the Royal Navy commissioned from John Thornycroft many motor torpedo boats during 1914–18, incorporating one or more steps. Most of them had no deadrise aft, and suffered from structural problems in way of the steps, due to the high slamming loads experienced by the hull bottom and the lack of continuity of structure inherent in the construction of this form. Stepped hulls undoubtedly gave superb speed/displacement results, but lost favour steadily because the structural problems could not be overcome if these craft ran at high speed over small waves.

Round-bilge types continued to be built, but these did not attain nearly the same sort of speeds as the unusual flat-bottom stepped yachts. Beam has increased throughout the years leading to better stability in a seaway at slow speeds, but higher wave impact loadings on the bottom. The development of

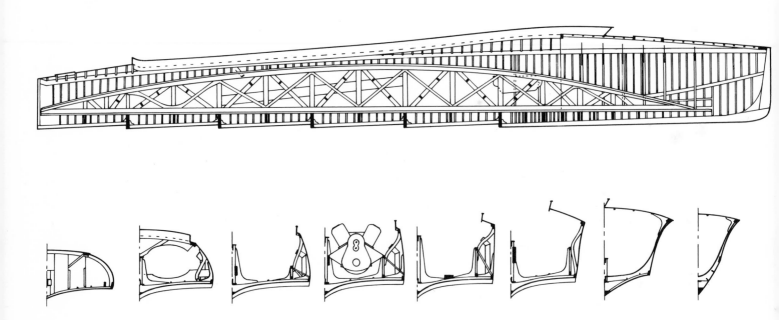

Fig. 3.4 (*above*). *Mapleleaf IV* in section and profile.
Designed and built by S. E. Saunders, she was the first boat
to attain 50 knots. Note the multiple steps in her bottom
and the complex structure associated with a stepped hull.

Fig. 3.5. Change of hull sections of fast motor boat over the
last seventy years. Notice the increase of deadrise angle
and the corresponding need for spray rails and greater
beam aft.

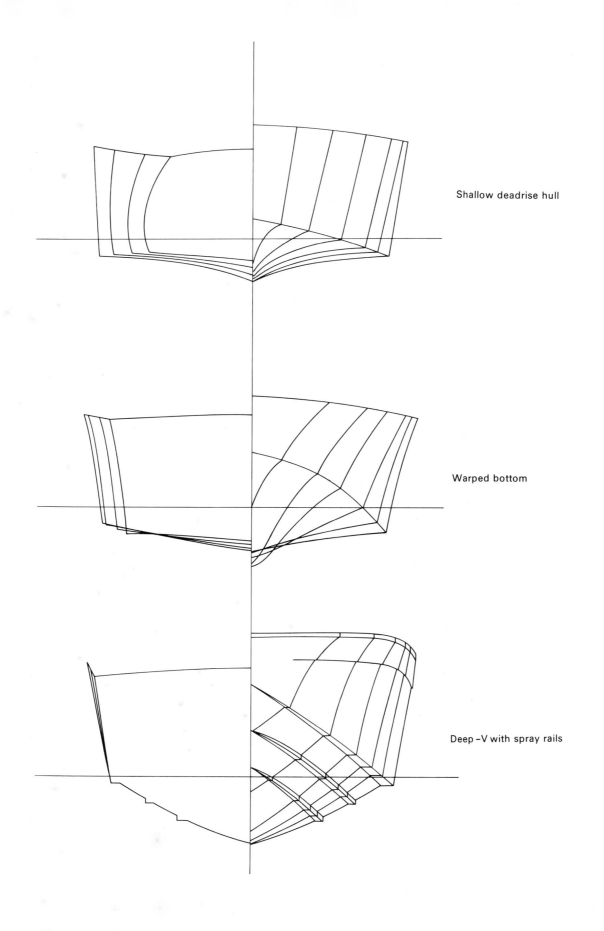

Shallow deadrise hull

Warped bottom

Deep -V with spray rails

Plate 7. *Turbinia* at speed. Her sleek lines can be seen in
Fig. 3.2. *Photo:* Beken

high-speed motor yachts over the past twenty years
has seen a steady increase in deadrise throughout the
hull bottom and the incorporation of spray rails.
Beam has also increased aft as deadrise has gone up,
to enable sufficient hydrodynamic lift to be
produced. The change of hull bottom shape can be
observed in Fig. 3.5. This is a generalisation as very
many weird and interesting craft have been built to
put a designer's theoretical ideas into practice.

Racing profiles have changed also as speed has
increased in an attempt to overcome the problem of
severe g loading on hull and crew, as the boat leaves
the water from the crest of a wave. The bow sections
have become longer and finer in an attempt to reduce
buoyancy in this area, so that the hull when landing
bow first on the next wave is not subjected to too
large a hydrodynamic and hydrostatic lift.

One of the major disadvantages of the flat-panel

Fig. 3.6. Hull section of modern fast motor yacht showing
complex curvature. The hollow at the chine helps keep the
boat dry and together with the spray rails, increases lift.

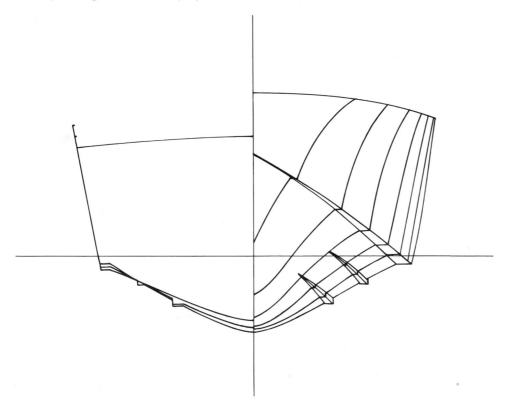

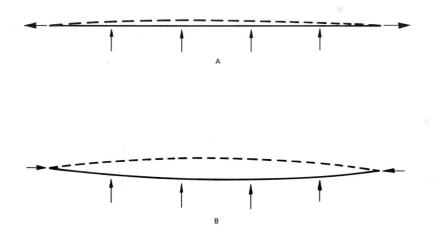

Fig. 3.7. End constriction on
plate under normal pressure
causing 'flip back'. The deflection
of plate A is limited by tensile
membrane stress set up over the
surface if the plate was initially
flat or concave to normal
pressure. Plate B, however, with
a small convex curvature
undergoes compression due to
end constriction causing it to
'flip back' to a concave shape
resulting in high stresses at the
fixing points due to the large
deflection.

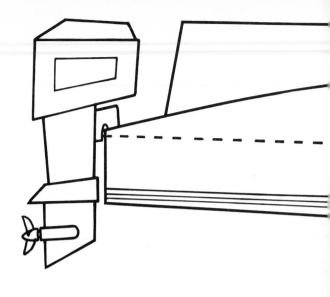

Fig. 3.8. Ram wing craft. Aerodynamic lift is provided by the bridging deck as well as the ram effect on the air flow between the deck and sea surface.

deep-V form is that if the hull should be heeled by the deadrise angle to the horizontal then this flat area is subjected to severe pounding on hitting the sea surface. Much work has been carried out on developing different bow forms both to lessen the g load and reduce the peak impact pressures. The fine knife-shaped bow section is particularly good as far as lessening g load is concerned, but it has the disadvantage that the yacht tends to be very wet and the hull also has tendencies to severe pitching and rolling when not planing; it is also more difficult to control in a following sea. Fig. 3.6 shows a hull form which is a good compromise both to lessen g load and roll, and to achieve hydrodynamic lift. The rounded sections also have the advantage that curvature in the shell itself gives some stiffness to the hull form. As will be indicated in Chapter 7, the major problem with GRP construction is that the material has low modulus, and some failures of motor-boat structures have occurred due primarily to the hull bottom being given a slight convex curvature. This form when subjected to high normal pressures tends to be forced into a curvature in the opposite direction due to the end constrictions on the panels (Fig. 3.7). The hull form shown has a complex curvature which would not be subjected to this type of tendency. The hollow in the chine area forces the spray outwards and downwards which both keeps the motor yacht dry and increases lift. Spray rails run from section 2 aft, to increase lift in the deep-V section further aft. These spray rails should be given very careful design attention as the pressure can be as much as 50 lb per sq in along the flat portion for a 50-ft motor yacht at 40 knots. In designing this hull form for GRP construction it is important that glass should be tucked well into the corners and resin drainage into these areas prevented, otherwise gel coat cracking will soon occur as the rails distort under pressure. Spray

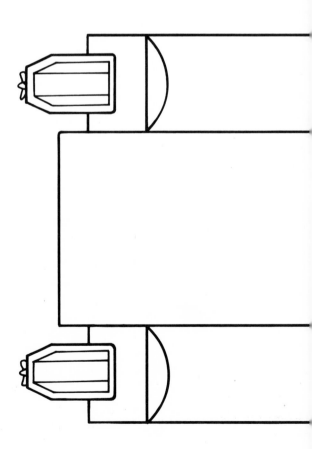

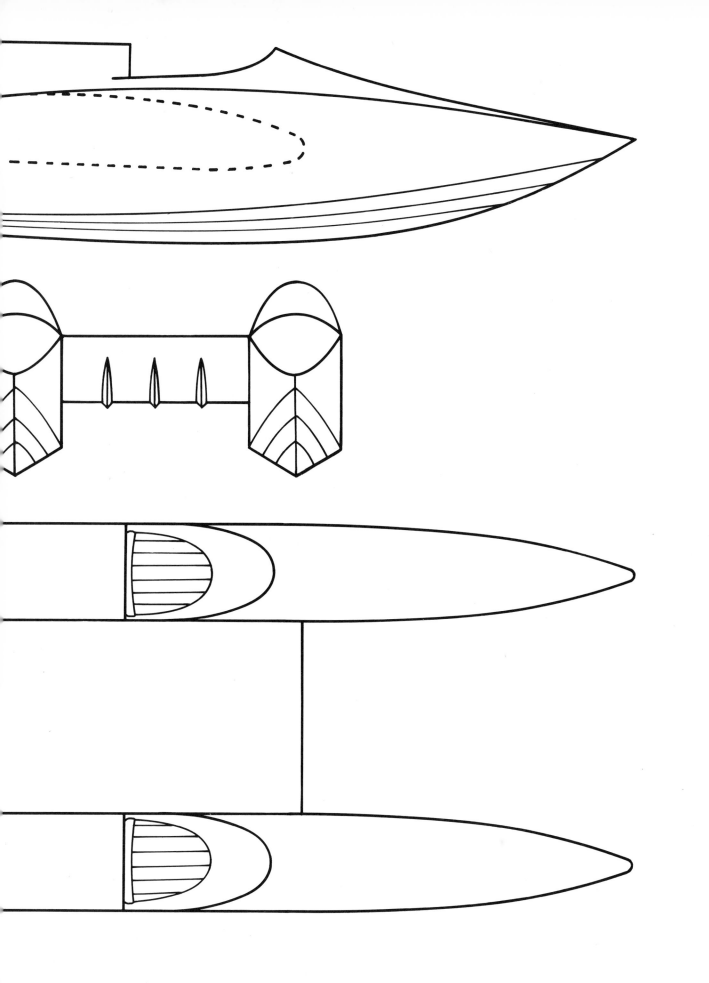

Plate 8. A modern deep-V planing craft. The impact loads on hitting the sea necessitate complex structural framing in order to achieve minimum weight. *Photo:* Beken

rails will also add a little to panel stiffness though they should never be regarded as equivalent to internal longitudinal stringers. The high degree of support offered by spray rails can be observed by watching the wake of a fast deep-V hull. In smooth water, if the rails are fairly closely spaced, the yacht may be observed to rise to successive rail levels as speed increases, with a distinct line left in the stern wash from each rail.

What are the likely developments in hulls, as indicated by present-day trends? The main resistance on the high-speed planing motor yacht is that due to skin friction and appendage drag. If it were possible to trap a layer of air along the hull surface while planing, frictional resistance would be decreased. This could be carried out by having a ram section as may be observed in small-circuit racing boats (Fig. 3.8). As speeds increase, skin friction on this type of section is decreased by air forced between the sea surface and the hull. An alternative would be to introduce an air scoop at the front of the boat with pipes leading to small openings in the hull bottom, forcing air along the skin further aft; it should be noted that any conventional propeller drive would be made far less effective as the air impinging on the propeller blades would lead to great loss of efficiency. However, this idea is highly suited to water jet propulsion as the water intakes could be housed in deep narrow scoops forward of the aeration holes thus helping to maintain drive even when the craft leaves the water surface.

Another application of this principle of air-entrapment is the introduction of a series of closely spaced longitudinal corrugations into the

Fig. 3.9. Corrugated hull sections for air entrapment. When at planing speed this hull would be riding on air trapped in the longitudinal grooves, reducing drag and giving a softer ride.

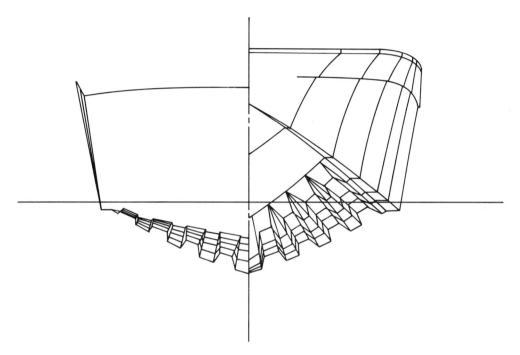

hull bottom which decrease in depth aft (Fig. 3.9). These have several advantages as not only is air trapped into the corrugations but also the bottom is given considerable rigidity and strength, requiring only transverse frames to be fitted. This hull form is extremely costly and difficult to build in wood or aluminium, but relatively simple in GRP when the bottom is laid up using strips of material of narrow width, enabling easy tucking into the corners. The normal deep V has the disadvantage that at low speeds it may tend to roll severely as the hull flops from chine to chine. But the hull form incorporating longitudinal corrugations has the added advantage that the corrugations act as roll dampers.

An even more interesting idea is to introduce transverse steps similar to those in the early high-speed planing craft like *Mapleleaf IV*. A further

decrease in hull friction is achieved as the bottom sections can be set at angles giving optimum lift throughout the hull length. Again, this is difficult to build in conventional materials but is straightforward with GRP.

The main problem with all types of planing craft is that of maintaining thrust in all sea states, as there will always be a tendency to leave the surface under certain conditions. Water jet propulsion is a highly efficient form for high speed, but again drive is lost when the scoops leave the surface. There are two possible solutions to this: the hull may be fitted with deep probes to catch the water (but these offer high appendage drag) or the hull can be fitted with a header tank so that, on leaving the surface, this reserve water is used for propulsion. This has the disadvantage that hull weight may be considerably

Fig. 3.10. Modern jet-propelled motor yacht. In harbour power is provided by diesel-driven propeller units which can be retracted to give a 'clean bottom' when jet propelled.

Fig. 3.11 (*right*). A medium-speed plywood motor yacht in profile, plan and section. A 60-ft craft of this type would give about 11 knots with an engine of only 40 h.p. and have low building costs.

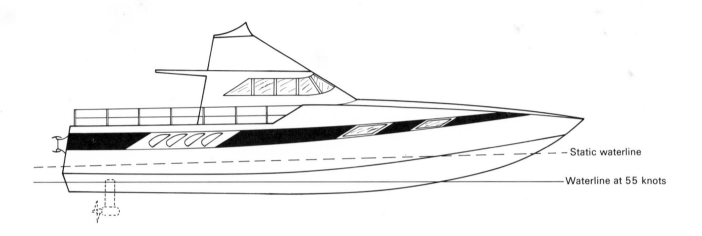

— — Static waterline

—Waterline at 55 knots

increased in order that a sufficient reserve may be carried. Very high-speed motor boats, such as the record breakers, eliminate this problem by using air jet propulsion. Perhaps the large luxury motor yacht of the future will be fitted with jet engines aft for high-speed cruising at sea, with a small diesel engine with a propeller mounted on a probe which can be drawn up into the hull to reduce appendage drag. This conventional drive would be used in harbour where the jet engine would be too dangerous. Jet engines have the great advantage that they are light for the power produced. For example 300 h.p. can be achieved from a jet engine while a diesel of the same weight would produce only 20 h.p. Also, using air jet propulsion, appendage drag from thrust units can be eliminated and the hull bottom designed without its influence.

A return can be foreseen of the long narrow motor cruiser which requires relatively little power in the speed range up to 13 knots. Typically a 60-ft cruiser having a beam of 7 to 8 ft can be powered by

a 40-hp diesel giving a comfortable 11 knots in a lumpy sea where the modern, beamy motor yacht of this length requires double the power and has a far more uncomfortable ride. This round-bilge dart-like form was a favourite of Herreshoff, and these types make ideal commuter or day boats. They cannot of course compete with the modern form for accommodation, but they can be built very cheaply if constructed of ply with a single chine. Fig. 3.11 shows a typical plywood mid-section for this type and the fine lines can be seen from the deck plan. A 60-ft hull built in ply costs less than half an equivalent luxury motor yacht. It is well known that this long, narrow hull form requires least propulsive force up to a $V/\sqrt{L}$ of 1.1. Above these speeds, the wide, flat aft sections, exhibited by many modern motor yachts, provide greater ease in planing. An anomaly occurs in the design of many motor yachts with a top speed of less than 15 knots as they are very often given the sections of the fast planing hull merely because it is current fashion. At lower speeds

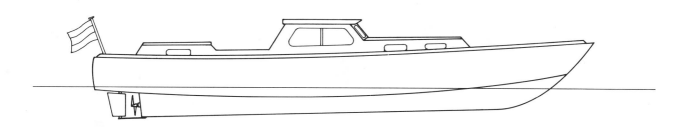

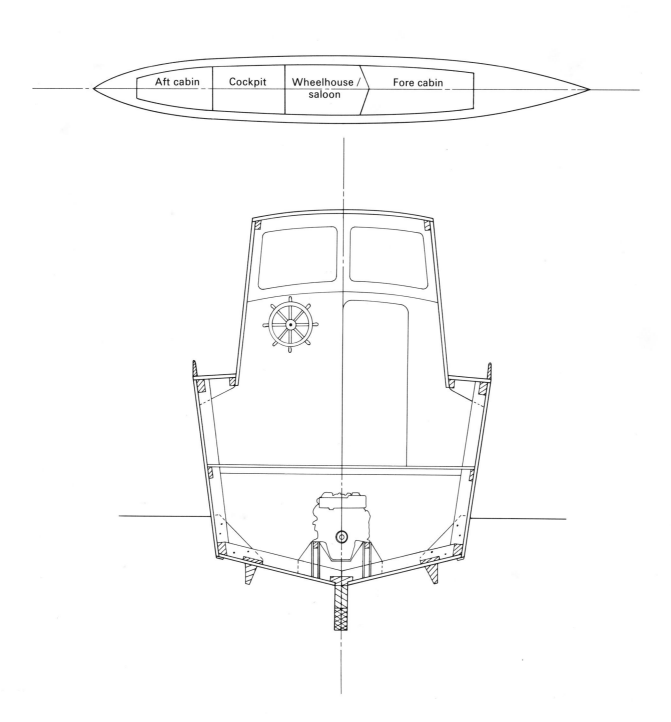

| Aft cabin | Cockpit | Wheelhouse / saloon | Fore cabin |

this hull form is less efficient than the round-bilge type, and much less efficient than the form described above. It is also very uncomfortable in a short seaway.

Now let us consider the development of a very high-speed craft, that is within the range of 50 knots upwards, for a 40-ft hull. The conventional high-speed craft is the planing monohull, usually of a deep-V form. These craft are supported on the water surface by hydrodynamic lift; however, they do displace a certain weight even at these speeds, unlike the hovercraft or hydrofoil. (In the case of the latter the only displacement is that of the foils themselves. Like all craft, hovercraft displace a certain volume of air, which of course may be ignored.) In a short sea our 50-knot, 40-ft boat will tend to become airborne, as it is impossible at these speeds to follow the wave contours because the accelerations in the vertical plane are too severe. This airborne effect is not desirable for the conventional hull form or for the crew. The main problem is how the severe g load may be reduced to an acceptable level as the hull hits the oncoming wave. Many different hull forms have been used in an attempt to solve this problem, including long and narrow round-bilge forms, stepped hulls, and catamaran types. The latest development is the deep V with spray rails, a characteristic observed in most offshore power boats of the racing type. The main aim is to control penetration into the oncoming wave at as slow a rate as possible, thus decreasing the deceleration g load. For example, if a power boat leaves the top of a wave with a downward acceleration of 2 g from rest (often the case because the stern gets accelerated upwards with the last of the wave) and the bow falls a height of 8 ft, the velocity of the bow section at impact is 32 ft per second. When a flat panel hits the surface, the hull can be brought to rest in as little as 6 in of water, creating a deceleration of 32 g. However, if the hull

can be made to penetrate the surface by, say, 16 in, then the deceleration is decreased to 12 g. This shows the necessity of allowing the hull slow penetration without of course complete immersion. The latest power-boat forms with long narrow fore-parts carry this out quite well as the area of impact is greatly reduced.

An interesting development for a high-speed monohull is a planing arm remaining in contact with the sea surface even as the hull body is airborne, thus preventing a big velocity in the downward direction as the hull meets the next wave. This could be coupled to a sea-sensor device using radio waves, feeding information to electric motors and operating a hydraulic ram to force the arm down on the surface at the correct time. It should be possible to maintain the hull at a constant level just in line with the wave tops in nearly all sea conditions. Very high speeds require such great power that it would be necessary to use wings to aid lift, thus reverting back to the flying-boat principle. Also, of course, very high speeds can be achieved below the surface where the air–surface interface has no effect on the craft. With the development of the very high-tensile steel and aluminium alloys, and the great power-to-weight ratio achieved in modern gas turbines, a flying boat deriving part of its lift from the sea surface and part from aerodynamic lift could be developed as a very fast motor yacht with extensive commercial or naval possibilities. Fig. 3.12 shows a high-speed motor yacht of this type, where aerodynamic lift is achieved by the short wings and hull superstructure but is not sufficient to take the craft completely clear of the surface. The wings have the benefit of reducing accelerations because the craft does not have the same tendency to follow the wave contours as conventional high-speed power boats.

Far more attention should be given to the aerodynamic resistance of superstructures as this

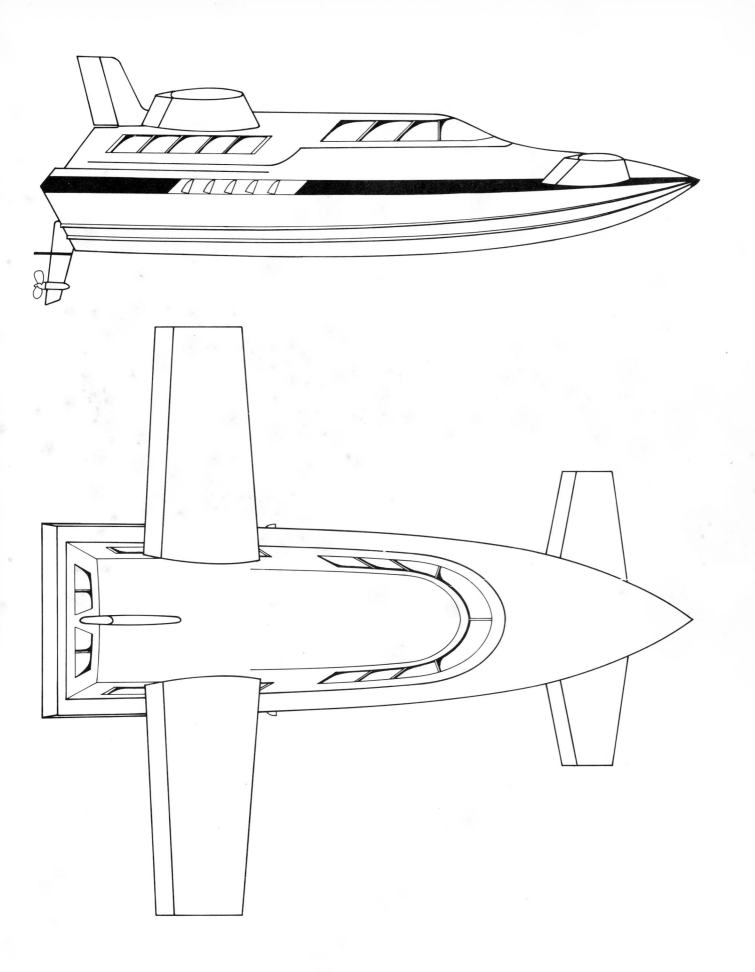

Fig. 3.14 (*right*). Different foil types. The requirements of a good foil system are basically, satisfactory transverse and longitudinal stability, high lift and low drag. Hydrofoils for use on lakes will have a different foil system from seagoing hydrofoils.

Fig. 3.13. Graph showing peak slamming pressure on the hull for varying waterline length and speeds.

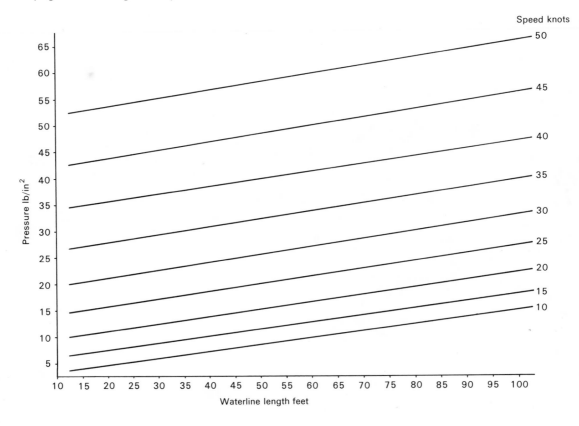

becomes an important factor in hull resistance at high speeds. Craft such as the *Brave* class patrol boats at 60 knots would have an air resistance in the order of 15 lb/sq ft on surfaces normal to the flow, but with careful streamlining for the pleasure motor yacht this could easily be reduced by 15 per cent.

As discussed earlier, the g load experienced by the hull and crew of the high-speed motor yacht is one of the most important limiting factors in the design of the hull structure and shape. Typical impact pressures for craft of varying speeds and lengths experienced on the bottom sections between station

two and midships are shown in the graph (Fig. 3.13). The magnitude of these forces on the hull structure due to slamming may be more readily appreciated when it is realised that a pressure of 20 p.s.i. over 1 sq ft of bottom is equivalent to a static load of 1·3 tons over that area of bottom panel! For this reason great care should be taken in designing the bottom hull structure and shape to lessen the possibility of failure under these huge impact forces. One interesting means of improving both the comfort of the ride and lessening stress is to mount all the internal structure flexibly using either rubber

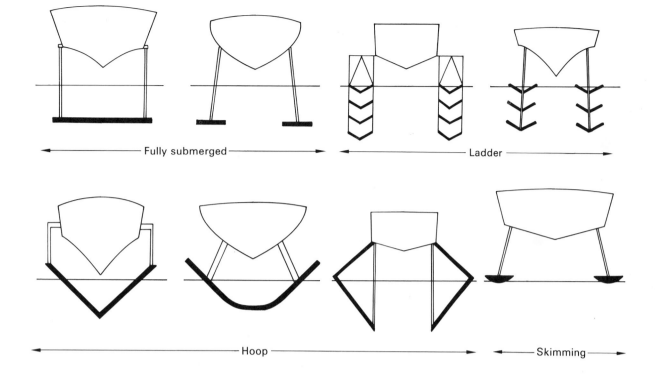

Fully submerged — Ladder

Hoop — Skimming

pads or springs and dampers. In motor yachts such internal suspension has the effect of increasing the time of deceleration, thus reducing the g force. This idea has been utilised in the sole of the *Brave* class fast patrol boat. Plates were fitted in the sole which were held by load and recoil springs to help reduce the shock inside these very fast craft. As the areas of sole suspended were very small this would have little effect in reducing the load on the bottom hull. If, however, the whole internal accommodation structure were to be mounted in this way, assuming this structure to be 20 per cent of the hull weight the impact pressure load on the bottom would be decreased by as much as 14 per cent. If the engines could also be mounted in a similar way, transmitting power through flexible hydraulic drives, the stress on the hull bottom would be decreased further.

Hydrofoils and hovercraft

A more recent solution to the g problem has been the development of the hydrofoil craft. Provided the body of the hull has sufficient clearance no great g-loads will be experienced, as the foils pass through the waves without much vertical motion. The ladder-

Hydrofoil type	L.O.A. (ft)	Loaded displacement (tons)	Speed (knots)	Engines/drive	H.P.
Bras D'Or (Canada)	151	200	60+	Gas turbine/prop	22,000
Hydrofin P20 (UK)	88	25	45	Diesel/prop	1,350
Bureau of Ships (USA)	180	500	80	Gas turbine/jet	6 × 20,000
Fresh 1 (USA)	53	15	100	Gas jet	18,000 lb thrust
Chaika (Russia)	86	15	47	Diesel/waterjet	1,200
P.T. 27 (Switzerland)	68	27	36	Diesel/prop	1,350
Aquabus 120A (Holland)	77	62	40	Gas turbine/prop	2 × 3,000
Denison (USA)	118	95	60	Gas turbine/prop	20,000

Table 3.1 Some recent hydrofoil types

foil type (Fig. 3.14) acts as a natural damper for hydrodynamic lift as the area of foil exposed can alter considerably without sudden change in lift. The heavier the hydrofoil craft becomes the more inertia it contains, and the less it will be subjected to severe accelerations in the short sea.

Although hydrofoil travel has only come into prominence over the last fifteen years, there is nothing new about this principle as it was first demonstrated in France by Count Alexander De Lambart in 1891. In 1906 Enrico Forlanini built and demonstrated a 40-knot hydrofoil on Lake Maggiore, and in 1918 Alexander Graham Bell and Casey Baldwin built a 5-ton ladder hydrofoil powered by two 350 h.p. Liberty aircraft engines, and reached a speed of 62 knots. The table below lists some of the features of many of the latest hydrofoils. Among them, the Canadian Navy's *Bras D'Or* is one of the fastest craft afloat today. Her speed has exceeded 60 knots at full load in 3- to 4-ft waves, and she has sailed foil-borne in seas up to 15 ft. At hull-borne speeds she is powered by a 2000 b.h.p. diesel engine through two reversible pitch propellers mounted on the upper part of the main foils. Her main engine is a 22,000 s.h.p. gas turbine driving through two supercavitating propellers, pod-mounted on the lower part of the foils. To ensure that the foil material was strong enough to support the high stresses imposed by this 200-ton craft, 18 per cent nickel sheet steel with an ultimate tensile strength of 250,000 lb per sq in was used. However, she did suffer many problems with this material, as it is very prone to stress corrosion cracking and hydrogen embrittlement, which is particularly prevalent under cavitating conditions. The vertical acceleration experienced in the bow in a force 5 sea state is far less than would be experienced in a fast conventional planing monohull. Such expensive craft built for military purposes provide design knowledge for

the future development of these types in the pleasure industry.

The major problem with hydrofoil craft in a tall steep sea is that of stability, if the hull is to ride high enough to clear the surface. This may be overcome to some extent by splaying the foils, but of course this has great disadvantages when docking as they may be damaged. An interesting solution to this problem is provided by the use of foils hinged at their connection with the hull, a hydraulic arm enabling them to be drawn in together on the centreline. Alternatively, if the foil continues up the boat's side then a hydraulic lifting arm could be used to draw the foil into the bottom of the craft (Fig. 3.15).

The hydrodynamic lift created by a given area of foil is far greater than that of an equivalent area of an aeroplane's wing simply because the density of water is 800 times as great, resulting in approximately 1/800 the area of wings for a given speed. Because the foils are supporting such a large weight over a small area their structural design has been one of the most difficult problems in the development of hydrofoil craft. If foils are fitted with trimming flaps, or can be bodily rotated, it is possible to eliminate both pitching and rolling, particularly if they are coupled to a gyroscopic sensor and either a sea probe in front of the craft or a radar wave detector. These flaps also have the advantage that the lift/drag ratio can be altered, and cavitation can be prevented on increased speed by reducing the angle of attack. Propeller installation becomes a problem in these high-rise craft and in the case of hydrofoils it should be made at the base of the foil to provide as deep immersion as possible at all times. Water jet propulsion using a scoop probe sited at the fore-end of the craft has great advantages (particularly if the weight penalty of a small reservoir can be accepted, enabling the probe occasionally to leave the surface causing no power reduction, and consequent change

Fig. 3.15. A hydrofoil having retractable foils. The foils and drive pad are arranged to slide up into the bottom of the hull allowing adjustment of ride height and reducing draught at low speeds.

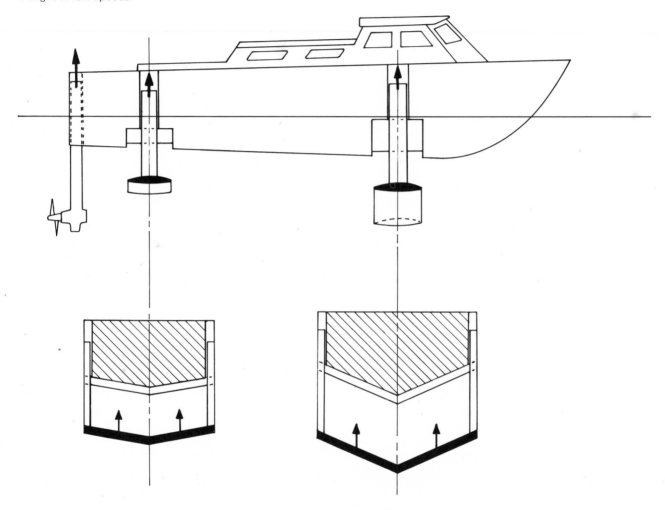

of motion). Hydraulic drive enables the propeller and its gearbox only to be mounted in the foils, thus no large appendage drag need be experienced as is the case if the engine itself has to be mounted at the base of the foil. Unfortunately, drives capable of delivering the required power are not yet available. In hydrofoil design we are faced with the natural law that displacement increases with the cube of length, while hydrodynamic lift increases with the square.

Thus, if the displacement of the craft is doubled the area of the foil should be increased four times for the same lift at a given speed; alternatively, the speed has to be increased, but this is generally more difficult.

An interesting and novel idea is a sailing hydrofoil incorporating an engine to maintain high speed when the masts are lowered. For low speeds when sailing the struts of the hydrofoil act as

Fig. 3.16. The transport speed range and resistance chart.
Hovercraft and hydrofoils.

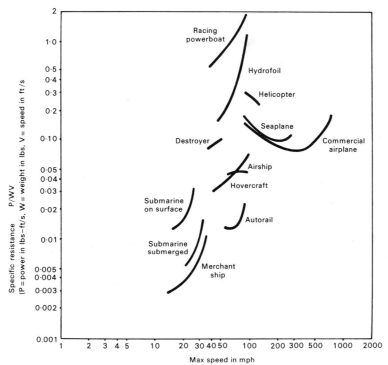

leeboards preventing excessive leeway and, when up on the foil, leeway is limited by the outward slope of the foils. This idea is particularly suited to a high-speed motor sailer as little power is required under motoring conditions.

There is a gap in commercial sea-air transport between 30 and 200 knots, i.e. between fast ship and air transport. A similar gap is shown in pleasure-craft transport, between about 40 knots and the 130 knots of light aircraft. This could easily be filled with hovercraft or possibly hydrofoils. A typical resistance chart for displacement and planing motor yachts, hydrofoils and hovercraft is shown (Fig. 3.17) for craft of about 60 ft. It will be observed that

the hovercraft requires far less power at the high-speed end of the scale than that of its counterparts. Typically, a double-seater hovercraft for speeds up to 50 knots requires a 750-cc petrol engine developing 50 h.p., equivalent to about a 20-h.p. diesel. For such a planing hull a 100-h.p. petrol outboard would be required, showing that the resistance for this type of craft is about twice that of the air-cushioned vehicle.

As the British were first in developing the air-cushioned vehicle, following Sir Christopher Cockerell's ideas and preliminary experiments at Lowestoft, the pleasure industry should take advantage of this great start and develop useful high-speed

Fig. 3.17. A resistance chart for various types of craft about 60 ft long. Notice how efficient the hovercraft is at higher speeds.

Fig. 3.19 (*right, below*). Hovercraft with 'two stage' skirt system. A large inflatable ring above the normal skirt increases the clearance under the main body of the craft.

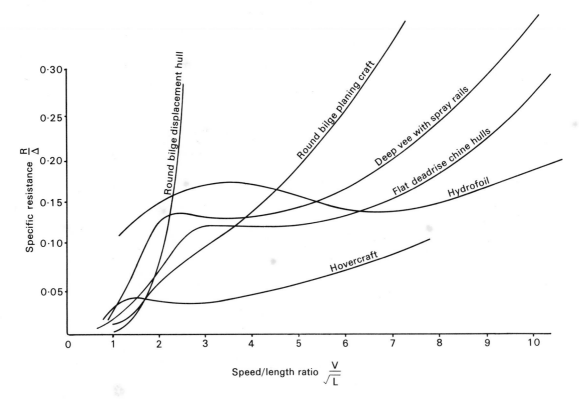

but low-power commuting craft of this type.

The major problem with present-day hovercraft transport is that in short, steep seas the ride becomes uncomfortable and even dangerous should air escape on one point of the skirt into the trough between waves. Three types of air-cushion arrangements are shown (Fig. 3.18); the simplest resemble an inverted cup but this type is unstable on all but a flat surface. The second requires less power to lift the craft as the jet is directed both downwards and inwards, helping to entrap a region of high pressure at the centre of the vehicle. This type again has the failing that on all but an even surface, the air can escape at one point causing instability. The third type uses a flexible double-wall skirt, thus projecting a concentrated high-pressure area around the circumference of the craft, and is the normal type of flexible-skirt hovercraft in use throughout the world today. This type is very much more stable on uneven surfaces but is limited in the sea conditions in which it can operate by the height of the flexible skirt. For a pleasure hovercraft of about 50 ft the skirt would be about 18 in deep, so this craft could not operate in seas of very short wave length if the troughs were deeper than the flexible skirt length. Fig. 3.19 shows a development in skirt design incorporating a deep flexible air-inflated ring above the skirt to give additional clearance to the hull itself should the wave heights exceed the inflated skirt depth. To improve comfort in hovercraft the accommodation area, as in

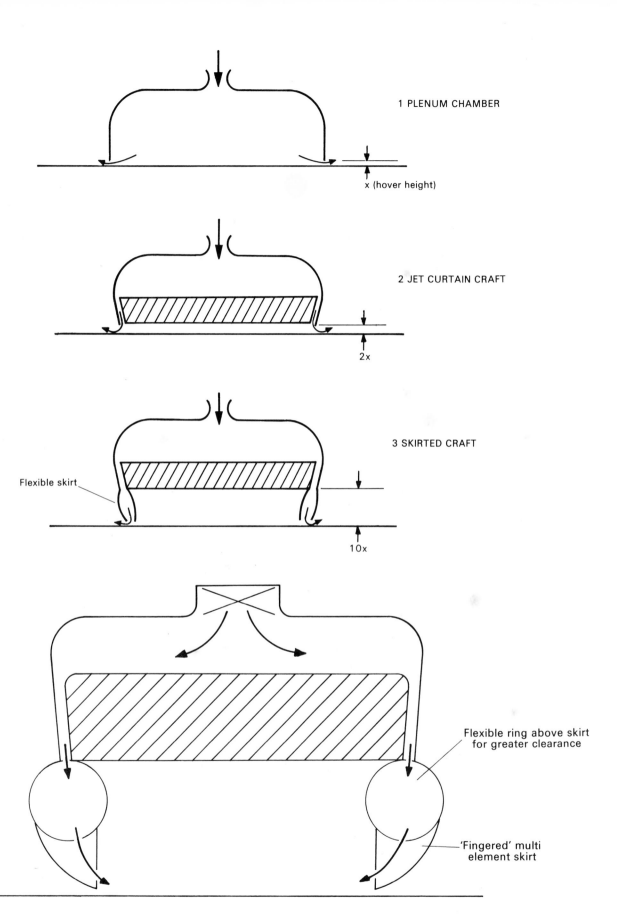

1 PLENUM CHAMBER

x (hover height)

2 JET CURTAIN CRAFT

2x

3 SKIRTED CRAFT

Flexible skirt

10x

Flexible ring above skirt
for greater clearance

'Fingered' multi
element skirt

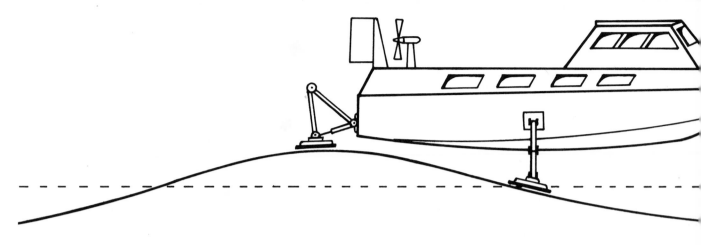

Plate 10. A typical side-wall hovercraft. Some ram effect is obtained at the bow section to reduce air loss under the cushion forward. *Photo:* Beken

Fig. 3.20. Leg-supported hovercraft. Levelling mechanism based on gyroscope, optical fix on horizon or oncoming wave sensor. Telescopic support arm supplies air flow to hover pads.

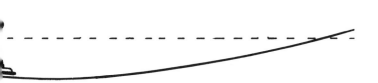

the high-speed motor yacht, could be flexibly mounted on a system of springs and dampers to reduce vertical accelerations.

Fig. 3.20 shows an idea for a large high-speed hovercraft using either jet or propeller propulsion. This craft would be supported on legs similar to those of hydrofoils, but at the base of each leg is an air-cushion pad. Provided the gap between the sea surface and the cushion pad is not excessive, the power required to lift a very heavy vehicle is surprisingly little; for example half a ton may be lifted on a cushion pad powered by a simple home vacuum cleaner, and thus very little force is required for horizontal motion. The arms of this futuristic vehicle would have flexible joints permitting the cushion pads to move vertically, and independently. A vehicle of this nature could be designed to travel over the sea surface in any type of condition provided the main hull were given sufficient sea

clearance, as the air would not escape suddenly from the support pallets as is the problem with the conventional hovercraft.

The hovercraft commonly observed is the side-wall type, which has the appearance of a large catamaran with flexible skirt at either end. Although the resistance for this type tends to be higher than for the all-flexible skirt vehicle, as the side walls are partially immersed to prevent air escaping down the sides, they travel more comfortably at reasonable speeds without the vertical thrust in action. For speeds in excess of 80 knots the skirt at the fore-end of this type of craft may be dispensed with if the jets at the leading edge are directed aft. This craft has a great similarity to the ram-planing hull in which air lift is obtained by the forward motion of the craft. In this type the skirt at the transom has to be carefully designed to prevent excessive air loss in this area.

4
Motor sailers

The motor sailer emerged during the 1930s when auxiliary engines became more reliable, compact and economical, permitting a powerful engine to be installed in a sailing hull which was then able to motor almost as well as a full-powered displacement craft, yet retained her sailing ability. This remains the criterion of the motor sailer, a type whose numbers have risen to perhaps one-third of the yacht total and which will continue to be popular, and in future develop high speeds under power. Sailing yachts which will plane under power have already been designed and built, but these are only one aspect of the motor-sailer type, which can at present be classified as

the well-powered auxiliary sailing yacht   (70/30)
the undercanvased but powerfully-engined
    yacht   (30/70)
the yacht reasonably fast under sail and equally
    able under power   (50/50)

Many motor sailers have large steering shelters, others carry big radar scanners at crosstree level, and most are now built with ketch rig, all of which creates windage and decreases windward ability. This tendency should be changed. The motor sailer, of all yachts, needs to have good windward ability, and the Bermudian sloop or cutter rig is desirable. This was recognised long ago by many American and Dutch designers, who helped to develop motor-sailer types with less excess beam and deckhouses than is exhibited by many of today's British designs. Numbers of large motor-sailing yachts are likely to be built as owners realise the genuine seagoing comfort and ocean-ranging potential of the type and, as size increases, the currently fashionable ketch rig will be replaced by the modern schooner rig on the larger craft, allowing the foresail and mainsail to be of almost equal area and keeping the sail handling within the crew's capacity.

The high potential speed of motor sailers, frequently punching to windward under sail and power with increased speed and pointing high to windward, requires the forward hull construction to be stronger than that of pure sailing yachts. For the same reason the masts, spars and rigging should be strong, as a wind blowing at 18 knots from ahead will, when motor sailing, be converted to a 30-knot breeze. Because of their close-windedness under combined sail and power, motor sailers will tend towards the use of fully battened sails, with optimum contour to suit the speed and weight of wind controlled by tensioning the battens with a system operated by a handle at the luff. Perhaps we will see more rapid rig development in this type as it is not restricted by any rating rules, while demanding good windward characteristics.

In contradiction to the general trend, many owners will prefer craft for long sea or ocean passages capable of sustained maximum speed under power at the expense of windward performance, and incorporating good engine installation practice. Continually rising costs have forced the lengths of all yachts to be carefully considered and often restricted, leading to motor sailers being frequently designed with insufficient length to exploit speed fully.

For comfortable long-passage making, future craft of this type will develop length at the expense of the present L/B proportions. More owners will desire speeds up to say 15 knots in motor sailers perhaps 45 ft long, having twin-screw machinery, moderate draught and a bow shape which will keep the deck dry at that speed through a short sea. The rig will be capable of reasonable speed on a reach or run, with ability on a close fetch.

Typical hull dimensions would be 48 ft overall × 42 ft waterline × 12 ft beam × 5 ft draft for craft of this type, to permit comfortable

Fig. 4.1. Use of furling gear on the mainsail. Although the lift on the mainsail will be reduced by this arrangement, the ability to reef or furl the sail quickly will result in the boat carrying more sail in light winds. (*See also page 68.*)

accommodation, arranged from forward as a forepeak store, two-berth cabin, bathroom and two large hanging spaces; a two-berth plus two occasional berths over, cabin; engine room with passageway between engines; galley and deck saloon which is half-sunk into the deck.

The steering position is amidships, over the engine room, with access from the cabin and door port and starboard to the deck. This places the helmsman almost amidship, with least motion, gives good forward visibility, and protects the wheelhouse from the worst of a breaking sea. Typically two 100-h.p. diesel engines drive through 2:1 reduction gears.

The ketch rig would be of modest area as windward work would be under power, or combined power and sail. The mizzen and mainsail are of almost equal size and a staysail and jib are set to reduce size to manageable areas for a minimum cruising complement of two. The masts are well stayed and the standing mizzen backstay will be a comfort in strong winds and heavy seas, with the yacht surging along on a course across the wind, engines running slowly and all sail set; the lee bow and quarter waves roaring and the knots reeling off the chart.

Equally, her twin screws and shoal draught enable small anchorages to be visited and in normal conditions she can make passages to equal the usual small-power cruiser, though her draught, breadth and form makes life aboard comfortable in comparison. Far from being regarded as a reversion in type, this style of motor sailer should be sought as the deep-sea ideal, rendered more efficient by modern equipment and materials.

The most important feature in the design of the rig for the motor sailer is that it should be handled easily by as small a crew as possible. It is useless designing a craft with a powerful large genoa or

high-aspect main, which, if caught out in squally conditions, requires a crew of three or four to hand the sail, for often the 40-ft motor sailer will be cruising with husband and wife, and perhaps children. Such a vessel should be capable of being handled by one person, for in bad conditions at night the wife will be left at the wheel to allow the husband to change sail with certainty of safety. Luff-furling gears permit easy reduction in foresail area and much reduce danger in changing to perhaps a storm jib, as the sail may be first furled and lowered without danger of flogging canvas and thrashing sheets. This idea of furling need not just be considered with the foresail, for the loose-footed mainsail or boomless main (Chapter 5) permits the luff to be fitted with a furling gear (Fig. 4.1). Although this spoils lift on the mainsail it is of more importance on the motor sailer to have a quick and efficient system of sail reduction, otherwise the rig tends to be far smaller than is desirable in light winds. This furling sail has the added advantage that it may be interchanged with headsails, allowing a more variable rig to be set at much reduced cost. Using this system for trade-wind work, double mainsails can be set with booms attached to the sides of the yacht, permitting the craft to be self-steering in following winds and requiring far shorter booms than if headsails are boomed out.

It is important for the cruising motor sailer to have transparent panels fitted in the headsails and mainsails to enable the helmsman to be left at the wheel singlehanded with good all-round vision, particularly in downwind work where a very large field of vision is obscured by the boomed-out sails. Perhaps in the future transparent cloths will be developed enabling the bottom few panels to be made up of this material.

To assist ease of handling, the motor sailer of the future might adopt a system of hydraulically-operated

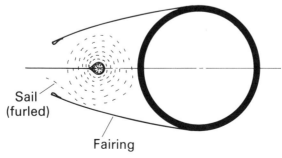

Sail
(furled)

Fairing

Fig. 4.1 (*continued*)

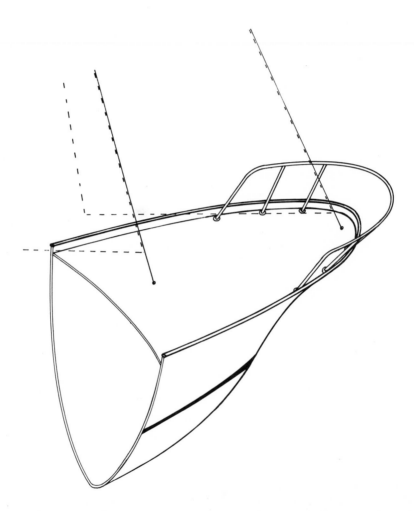

sheet winches powered from a central motor. This system would consist of a main pump with drive units for halyard winches housed inside the mast with the drums mounted on the exterior or forward of the cockpit on deck, and similarly the sheet winches could be driven by a flick of a switch. Provided the main driving motor is of sufficient power, the windlass on the foredeck could also be run from the same system. If the foresail sheet winch is mounted in the centre of the cockpit the sheets could be made a continuous loop permitting them to

remain on the winch and, when going about, the hydraulic winch is simply reversed.

Ideally masts in a motor sailer are stepped on deck. Although this requires a slightly greater mast section than for a keel-stepped spar for the same sail area, it allows the rig to be lowered by the crew and reduces fitting-out costs. If two of the shrouds, one each side, are positioned so that they remain under tension as the mast is lowered in the tabernacle, then clearly no control during lowering is required from the sides of the yacht. The mast can be lowered then

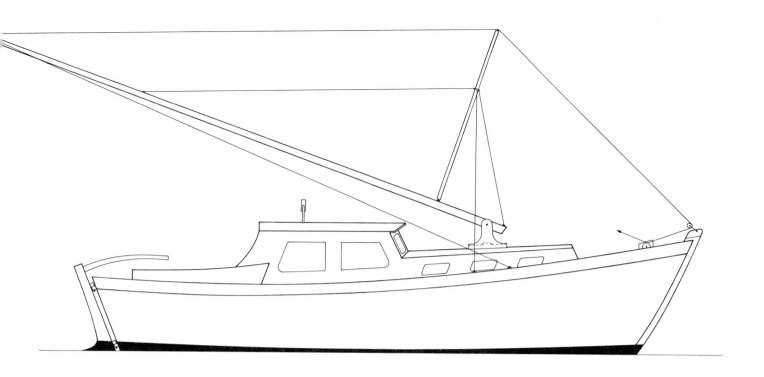

by one person using the foredeck winch and, if necessary, a main or spinnaker boom to achieve the best leads (Fig. 4.2).

When sailing in the tropics the sun about mid-day can be very intense, thus the well-designed cruising motor sailer should be equipped with a framework which can be attached to the mast and shrouds enabling a canopy to be fitted over nearly the full length of the yacht. It is not enough to have this sun shield over only the helmsman, as considerable temperatures may be recorded below deck due to prolonged radiation. For the cruising yacht sailing the tropics, a useful and relatively simple idea is to fit sprinklers driven by a sea-water pump which can be switched on periodically to cool the decks. This system must be fitted and used with some caution as such heating, wetting and cooling can play havoc with timber-laid decks. It is desirable to have deck, deckhouse and topsides painted in light colours in order to reflect as much radiation as possible. For the yacht sailing in more temperate conditions the fully protected wheelhouse has much to recommend it. Most people buying motor sailers do so in an attempt to achieve the best of several

worlds. It is acceptable to the helmsman of the racing yacht to be exposed in a shallow open cockpit for his watch, which would normally last for four hours at the most. The cruising helmsman does not wish to be out in cold wet conditions watch after watch if he is sailing for pleasure rather than racing. A system with all the sheets led to winches via blocks inside the wheelhouse, perhaps half-sunken to avoid excessive windage, allows the helmsman to sail the yacht singlehanded and to put about without waking up the crew. However, attention should always be given to sheet leads as it becomes annoying and very tiring if, every time a sail boat puts about or comes tight up into the wind, blocks jam or start to bang on decks above the berths.

The present trend with the modern offshore racing yacht is to have flush decks and small toe rails. This is not the best deck layout for the cruising motor sailer as vision and light below are severely restricted by flush decks, and small toe rails give very little security on deck. High bulwarks with of course sufficient freeing ports give a greater feeling of protection when going forward, particularly with stanchions and guard wires run along the top. These

Fig. 4.3. The modern bow form for motor sailers. Note that
although the hull is very fine at the waterline the foredeck is
wide in way of the forestay and pulpit. Dryness is assured
by the flared bows.

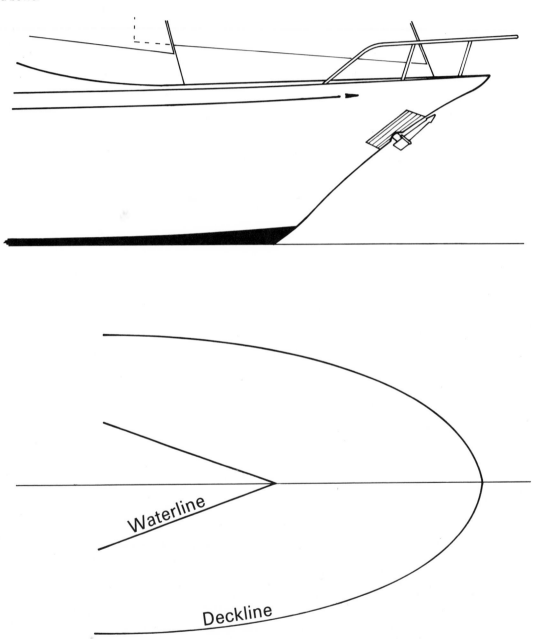

Plan view

guard wires need be only 2 ft above the top of the bulwark as opposed to 3 ft above the open deck. Bulwarks also help to keep the foredeck dry when going to windward in a short sea. Because of the apparent increase in freeboard when viewed in profile, great care should be taken with the aesthetic appeal of the motor sailer. A change in colour for the bulwarks and plenty of sheer help to make the high freeboard less apparent. Deckhouses enable headroom to be increased and permit good all-round vision through ports and windows. They also help to break up the sheer line in profile which often gives more character to the yacht.

Going forward in this type of craft is easier than in the modern offshore racer with flush decks which give little sense of security under severe conditions. Ideally, side-deck widths should not be less than 15 in (38 cm) for the larger motor sailer, as this will permit one to turn round easily when walking along the sides. The guard wires observed on many offshore racers provide no security and are often dangerous as the top wire tends to be the height of the knee so that on stepping backwards one is caught behind the knee and tipped overboard.

On light-displacement offshore racers the trend has been to carry very little cable and small anchors, often stowed in inaccessible places to attract as little weight penalty as possible. This is undoubtedly an unhealthy trend, though the offshore racing yacht's ability to creep to windward off a lee shore under almost any conditions has meant that few disasters have occurred. The motor sailer, however, does not point so high and will often have a less experienced crew aboard. Thus it is of prime importance that it should be able to hold at anchor in severe conditions on a lee shore should the engine break down. To permit this, the anchors should be accessible and of sufficient weight to give high holding power. Sufficient chain cable should be stowed aboard as under severe conditions with a smooth rocky bottom, approximately six to eight times the depth of water in scope of chain cable is required. Very often the worst type of bottom for holding the anchor is found on a steep-to shore. Thus, a yacht caught with this type of lee shore will need at least 30 fathoms of cable out to hold it in 5 fathoms of water. For the larger motor sailers, the 'clipper' bow has the great advantage that the anchor can be self-stowing in a hawsepipe into the bow, permitting very quick letting-go. The forward lines of a yacht with a clipper bow very often have to be flared in the topsides to achieve fairness. But this has the added advantage that the foredeck can be made wide in way of the forestay and windlass, and also the foredeck will tend to remain dry. Motor sailers usually pitch violently when motoring to windward in a sea. The typical outreaching form of clipper bow now used in many yachts dampens this and throws spray outboard but, in larger motor sailers, designers will increasingly adopt a modified form (Fig. 4.3) which has a sharp entry up to the outward curve of the lower stem, swelling to a rounded fullness of section above that to a half-elliptical shaped deck plan at the stem. This provides additional buoyancy, dampens pitching, allows adequate structural arrangements in way of a hawsepipe and improves deck space at the stemhead which is always encumbered with forestays, mooring fittings, stowed headsails and warped cable leads to the windlass or mooring bitts.

Three-bladed controllable-pitch propellers enable much greater propeller diameter to be achieved and efficiency to be increased at all revs. With this increased diameter the reduction gear box will very often have to be increased to reduce shaft revs. This permits greater ease in manoeuvring at slow speed with much increased thrust: instead of the normal 2 : 1 reduction box fitted in the average motor sailer,

Fig. 4.4. Profile of modern 84-ft motor sailer *Blue Mermaid*.

or direct drive in the case of the racing yacht to keep the propeller and shaft diameter to a minimum, the large-diameter variable-pitch propeller requires 3 or 3·5 : 1 reduction. The slower shaft revs and increased shaft diameter will often help to reduce vibration and noise from the sterngear. Although the drag of the variable-pitch propeller when sailing may be minimised by feathering the blades, the lower shaft revs and subsequent increase in diameter and size of brackets will have a detrimental effect on performance if a fin and skeg type is adopted. The long-keel motor sailer with propeller aperture in the deadwood area or rudder experiences no such increase in appendage drag as little of the shaft is exposed.

To assist steering, the rudder on the motor sailer can be partially balanced by having some of the rudder area in front of the stock. Although this system does not lead to maximum turning force for a given area (maximum efficiency is achieved by having a higher aspect rudder behind a skeg as far aft as possible), the area and subsequent frictional resistance is of less importance in the modern motor sailer. The rudder and propeller can be protected by running a continuation of the keel shoe to form a lower rudder pintle, removing much of the bending force from the rudder stock. This long-keeled motor sailer has the added advantage that it is easier to ground and dock, unlike the modern deep-fin racing sailboat which can be a great headache to the boatyard without a travel lift, and may also be both uncomfortable and dangerous if caught aground unintentionally with a falling tide.

One necessity, sometimes ignored by many designers of the modern motor sailer, is ease of access to the engine and also provision for its removal. This is important particularly for the cruising motor sailer as opposed to the fast modern sailboat, as it should be assumed that 50 per cent of

sea time will be under power, and the engine relied upon to make Sunday evening deadlines. The centre-cockpit motor sailer permits a large hatch to be fitted in the cockpit sole above the engine compartment, enabling both engine and gearbox to be easily hoisted out. The larger motor sailer having twin engines mounted aft for minimum sound and vibration, using V-drive transmission, can be fitted easily with a removable hatch in the aft cockpit, or a bolted watertight section fitted to the transom.

A modern design for a fast 84-ft motor sailer of the future, the *Blue Mermaid*, is illustrated (Figs. 4.4 and 4.5). She represents the ultimate in ocean-going efficiency and comfort combined with moderate draught for entering small harbours and shallow waters. The GRP hull has a fine outreaching bow of a shape to maintain a dry foredeck under most conditions and the powerful flat run ensures speed and stability under sail and power, besides flattening the wake and aiding downwind speed. A modern fin and skeg arrangement, shown in the profile, gains optimum windward performance, so that she could make fast trans-ocean passages. A long keel drawing 6 ft 6 in for shallow draught operation could be designed enabling her to creep up estuaries. Twin centreboards, housed between tanks forward and aft, would be adopted with this version.

Accommodation rivals a motor yacht of comparable size and the large deck saloons provide the excellent dining and lounge space with a clear view of activities in an anchorage which is so enjoyable a part of yacht cruising.

The rig is a modern schooner, described in Chapter 5. Of almost equal height, the masts lend a look of power to the sleek hull and bring into scale the full-height deckhouses. Headsails include a quadrilateral jib, and this schooner is capable of being driven at speed under most weather and sea conditions by a modest crew. When desired, the

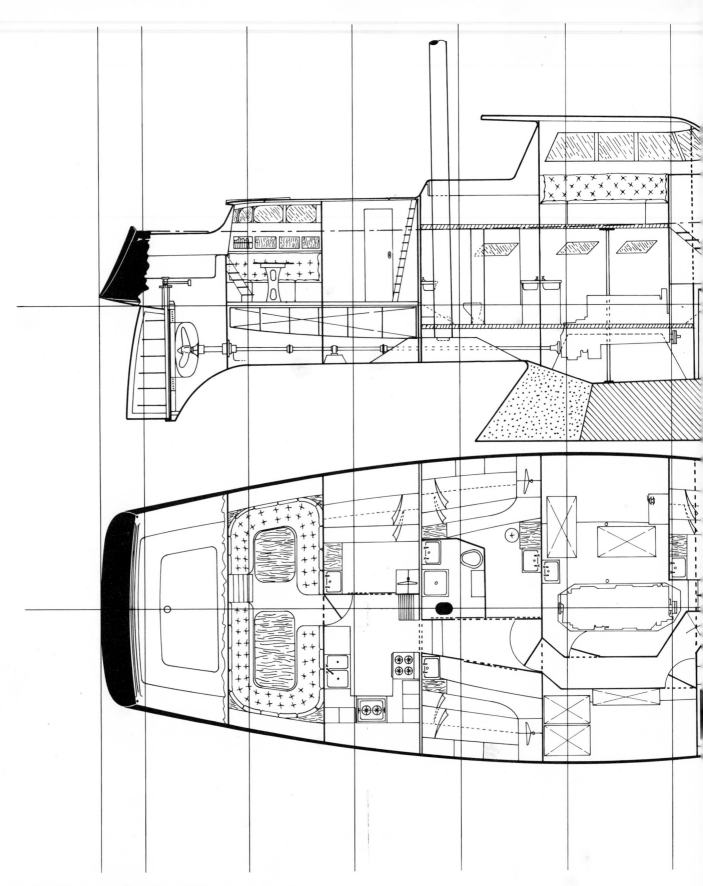

Fig. 4.5. The modern 84-ft motor sailer *Blue Mermaid,*
profile and general arrangements. It can be seen that the
raised portion of superstructure provides a spacious deck
lounge with all-round visibility and allows full standing
headroom in the engine-room below.

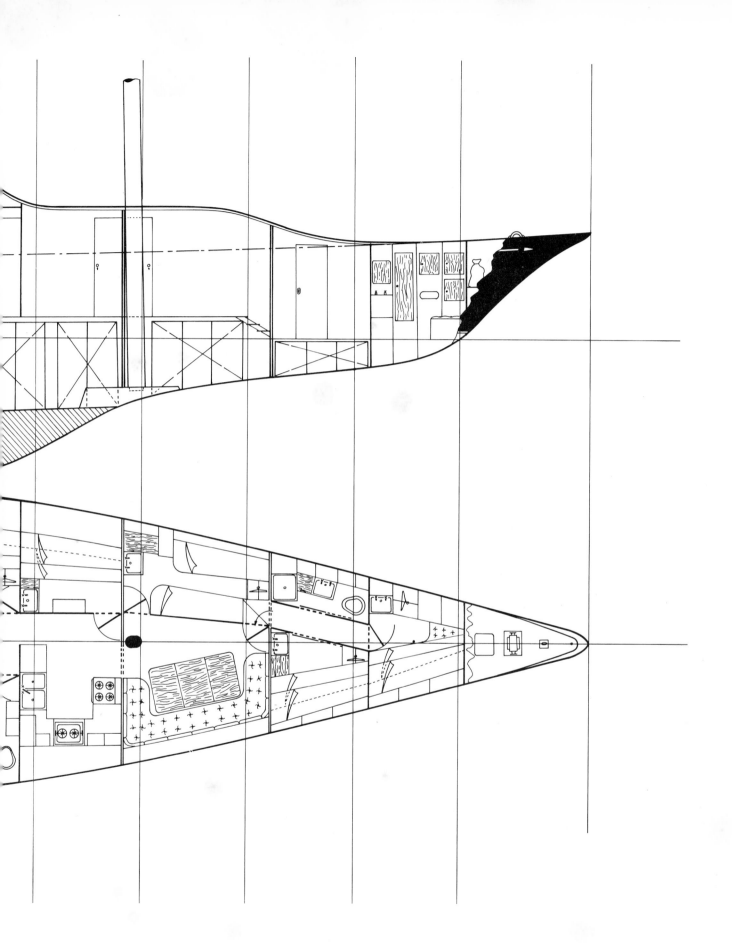

Fig. 4.6. Profile, general arrangements and deck plan of 86-ft twin drop plate schooner based on Baltimore clipper schooner. The very shallow draught permits this craft to sail into harbours that would normally never be attempted by a craft of this size.

300-h.p. diesel engine can thrust her along at 14 knots in smooth water, or sail and power will maintain high speed with fine control in strong winds and a heavy sea. The fortunate owner of this schooner will have a world-ranging cruiser with the accommodation of a home afloat. In the past large windows such as those shown fitted in the deckhouse would have been thought unseamanlike. However, the development of modern plastics and toughened glass makes them as strong as the surrounding structure. This trend will develop to enable whole deckhouse tops to be finished in translucent material, with electrically operated internal shutters closing across when desired, e.g. alongside quays, in strong sunlight or at night.

Such a schooner makes a fine charter yacht and Fig. 4.5 illustrates an arrangement for this purpose. A permanent crew of three or four live forward in two double cabins with a bathroom provided for their use. An insulated transverse bulkhead partitions them from a range of three double-berth guest cabins to starboard, served by a bathroom, well-equipped galley and dining saloon capable of seating six in comfort.

A stairway leads up to the deck lounge and another down to an alleyway bypassing the engine room. Aft of this are three more spacious double-berth cabins served by a bathroom and galley which opens on to a 'great cabin', dining/lounge, which extends the full breadth of the yacht. Its U-shaped settees and hand-rubbed Honduras mahogany tables lit by gimballed lamps make this a snug setting.

The helmsman's position at the forward end of the deck lounge is equipped with hydraulic steering gear and fully instrumented with log, wind speed and course instruments. A comfortably upholstered steering chair with adjustable seat and back enable long tricks at the helm to be enjoyed and the helmsman has excellent vision forward, on each side

and aloft, through the large deckhouse front windows and a transparent panel in the roof. The thrill of sailing one of these yachts in a breeze will be akin to handling a J-class yacht of the 1930s.

The planing motor sailer will soon be a practical craft. Lighter hull construction and finishing materials which will also have ample strength, combined with improved power/weight ratios of engines, will enable speeds up to 25 knots to be attained under power. Hull form might be a stepped chine with convex bottom having sailing stability and roll damping under power, combined in a keel-mounted foil at about 5 ft below the bottom, maximum draught being 6 ft. The twin sterndrives will retract into a watertight compartment when sailing, and the bottom will be closed by a hydraulic panel, preserving sailing efficiency. This craft will also have planing potential off the wind in strong breezes, when the deep, transom-hung rudder will tend to arrest broaching. Increasing use of semi-rotating, horizontal plane sails will be applied ideally to the planing motor sailer, where they can be stowed on the retracting masts discussed in Chapter 5, flat on the cabin tops, or partially raised to act as sun awnings.

The operation of charter yachts for cruising under sail and power has grown tremendously during the past 20 years, particularly in the Caribbean and Mediterranean. This trend will continue to expand, particularly in the field of 'character' craft — thoroughly efficient sailing vessels of modern construction and accommodation, but styled after sailing ships of the romantic era.

Fig. 4.6 is typical of these appealing craft. The future requirement will probably demand sailing vessels capable of accommodating twelve guests and a crew of four for ocean or inshore cruising charters. Future charterers will expect skindiving equipment and water ski boats which will be stowed aboard in

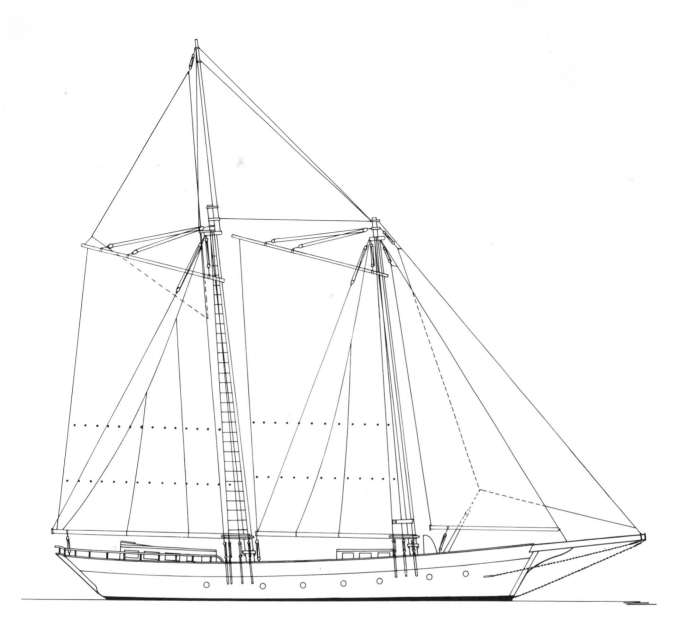

big deck lockers. The draught should be restricted as little as possible and for a waterline length of 70 ft a 6 ft maximum could be achieved, which would enable her to creep under power into secluded coves and lonely gunkholes far from crowded marinas and noisy harbours. Large centreplates however will allow an increase in draft up to 11 ft for windward work. This twin-plate fore-and-aft arrangement gives the advantage of balancing the centre of lateral resistance with the selected sail arrangements. This modern type has ancestors in the Baltimore clipper schooners, fast merchant, privateer and sometimes slave schooners out of Chesapeake Bay which later influenced many of the designers of the sailing ships of the mid-19th century 'Clipper' era. They were renowned for speed and weatherliness; exciting vessels to sail and inspiring affection among their crews. Although the charter yacht of the future looks very traditional, all the gear associated with modern yacht handling will be utilised to sail with limited crew and in greater safety. The internal arrangements will incorporate the latest materials and arrangements so that living aboard becomes a luxury.

Typical hull dimensions of 86 ft × 22 ft × 11 ft depth allow spacious cabins and a half-sunk deck saloon behind 2 ft-9 in bulwarks with a separate galley forward. The 22-ft beam affords plenty of

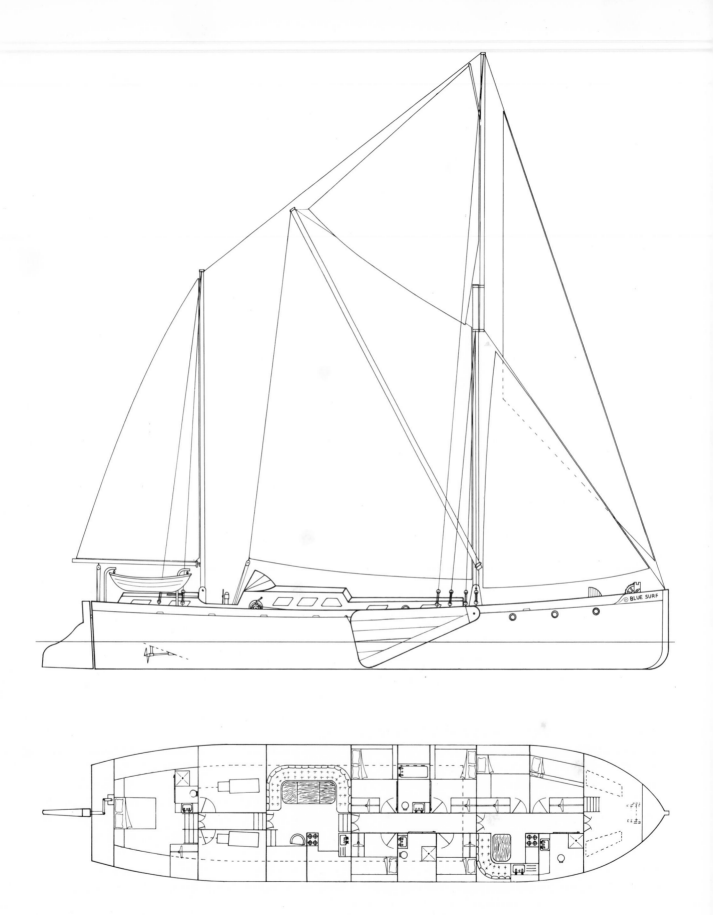

BLUE SURF

deck space for working ship or sun lounging, at sea or in harbour, and the broad counter stern gives buoyancy aft and enables the motor boat to be slung across it in davits. The schooner rig gives great flexibility of sail areas to suit differing weights of wind and all sails can be handled from the deck as the jib can be fitted with furling gear. Both masts rake with suggestive speed, typical of their ancestry, and the hull's springing sheer is prolonged by a well-steeved bowsprit. A Terylene net catches headsails when lowered, and besides safeguarding those working on the bowsprit, provides a comfortable lounging place during passages on summer seas.

Twin 140-h.p. diesels drive through shafts on either quarter providing 11 knots maximum speed and good manoeuvring under power in confined waters. The aim would be to achieve seaworthiness with shoal draught and to retain the feel of an ocean-ranging vessel. As a sail training ship, an alternative rig could be provided for these vessels.

Cruising yachtsmen visiting other craft larger than their own often exclaim 'Why, she's as big as a barge!' However, there is no reason why the barge should not be used as a basis for a modern cruising motor sailer. The high block coefficient will ensure spacious accommodation below and large initial stability with shallow draught. This type makes an ideal long-distance cruiser for those contemplating passage-making, for sail-training organisations seeking a 'shippy' but relatively inexpensive training ship, and for yachtsmen fond of spacious craft capable of exploring coastal or shallow waters while still retaining the ability to make ocean passages. Typical dimensions would be 88 ft overall × 20 ft beam × 4 ft draft of hull with centreboards (or leeboards) up, extending to 9 ft with boards down.

This type is particularly suited to heavy GRP construction as displacement is of little consequence.

The cost of construction is relatively cheap as complex framing is eliminated due to the heavy shell. Alternatively, the slab sides and bottom permit ease in steel construction as little plate-forming is required. The rig may be spritsail or gaff totalling 3500 sq ft of working sail. Her appearance could be striking and seamanlike, both qualities often lacking in much contemporary yacht design.

This 88-footer can provide luxury accommodation with spacious day lounge, sleeping cabin, full-scale bathroom, dressing room and entry lobby leading to a suite which is fitted with enormous wardrobe and stowage space (Fig. 4.7).

A proposed typical arrangement calls for three double-berth guest cabins which are of good proportions, also a large dining room flanked by a well-equipped galley and bulkheaded off forward for the crew's accommodation comprising a captain's cabin, steward's cabin and a double cabin for seamen. For the fastidious owner, living aboard for long periods, air conditioning and hot-water heating systems can be installed without intrusion on living space. The galley has space for a big Aga stove or large oil-fired range, if required, and water and fuel tanks are built into the hull. As weight is no problem furnishings can be lavish giving the comfort of a small ship combined with the advantages of shoal draught. Alternatively, she can be arranged as a training ship with accommodation for a captain, two watchkeeping officers, two other officers aft, and sleeping and messing accommodation for twenty trainees with a large galley and ample washplace.

The bowsprit has been kept to a moderate length. Aluminium masts and spars, synthetic sails and running rigging, plastic blocks and modern methods of standing rigging combine in a light, strong and efficient rig which would have surprised the old sailing bargemen. It enables the craft to be sailed readily by amateur and often inexperienced crews. A squaresail, hoisted aloft when required, otherwise stowed along the bulwark, is carried for trade-wind sailing or long runs. The squaresail is set in two parts, from the deck, with no need to anyone to work aloft. Those who have surged over ocean seas under a squaresail will appreciate its superiority over a spinnaker in those conditions. Two large steel centreboards can replace the leeboards of the originals. The cases are incorporated into cabin partitions and are unnoticeable on board. When lowered the two centreboards ensure good course-keeping at sea but with the forward board half raised she will tack readily. A spacious steering cockpit aft gives the helmsman a clear view forward and aft. There is ample deck space for handling sails and gear and a 16-ft dinghy and a 12-ft sailing dinghy are carried in chocks on the after deck, handled by a derrick from the mizzen. The Danforth bower anchors can be carried in hawsepipes and a hand electric or hydraulic windlass can be fitted. The auxiliary engine installation may be either single or twin screw. A typical twin 120-b.h.p. installation will achieve 10 knots on full power. The spacious engine room permits easy maintenance of the engines, auxiliary machinery and electrics; a rare luxury in a modern yacht.

As a type the motor sailer has the greatest potential for development in yacht design. Continuing improvement in engine power/weight ratio and reduction in size for a given power will enable designers to produce significant improvements in accommodation and the present concept of the auxiliary will have much in common with the 50/50 motor sailer of the future.

5
Spars, rig and sails

As the engine is to the motor yacht, so sails and spars are to the sailing yacht, and equivalent attention should be given to their development to use wind power efficiently. During the past forty years their design has lagged behind hull form and construction changes. It is not sufficient to hoist a triangular sail up a circular or oval-sectioned mast merely because this custom has become well established. More effort should be made to produce a high lift/drag ratio for the rig as a whole and one should not consider the mast just as a supporting member for the sail.

Ignoring the effect of rating rules, mast development should be influenced by the properties of the materials and the aerodynamic qualities required. At present, masts are designed as members purely to hold up the sails, and their aerodynamic effect is detrimental to that of the sail. As they are compression members with some degree of lateral force imposed by way of the boom (forestay in the case of the $\frac{3}{4}$ or $\frac{7}{8}$ rig) and a very small uniform lateral pressure due to the sail itself (Fig. 5.1), their design is governed by Euler's formula, i.e.:
$P/A = CE\pi^2/(L/r)^2$. Here P is the total compressive load, A the area of section, E the modulus of elasticity, L/r the slenderness ratio, and C the coefficient of constraint depending on the end conditions, e.g. whether the mast is stepped on deck or on the keel with the deck supporting at some distance from the base. Thus, for a given material the modulus of elasticity is fixed, and assuming the load to be fixed, the area of section, slenderness ratio and coefficient of constraint may be juggled to give the optimum compressive support for minimum aerodynamic resistance. For instance, one approach would be to reduce the area of section and slenderness ratio of the whole spar, but, in effect, to divide the whole into lesser lengths by the introduction of numbers of spreaders, diamonds and

shrouds. So although the aerodynamic resistance of the main compression member is reduced, that of the whole rig might, unknowingly, be increased by virtue of the rigging resistance. In designing this type of spar, often thought is not given to attempting to attain some aerodynamic lift from the compression member, but merely to keeping the projected area to a minimum.

The slenderness ratio factor L/r is dependent upon the length of the column and the least radius of gyration. Rearranging Euler's formula as $P = ACE(r/L)^2\pi^2$ the compressive load supported for a given area of section may be greatly increased by reducing L or increasing r. Assuming the length of the mast to be fixed, r has the greatest effect on the load-carrying capacity of the mast. However, in increasing r we are normally increasing the aerodynamic resistance of the spar as the inertia of section is raised. An interesting solution to this problem is that of the mast shown (Fig. 5.2), which has been tested and proved to be very successful in dinghy racing.

The tri-spar consists of a central-plate compression member with two smaller vertical members at the side joined with a framework of horizontal triangular plates and cross-lattice. The cross-sectional length and breadth are about twice those of a conventional mast and the design permits construction from standard flat sections and sheet. The construction does not offer excessive windage, and tests show that the sail is closer-winded, developing more drive than with conventional rigs. While frictional resistance is probably higher, the increase in driving force is proportionately greater and hence the angle of attack is improved. In addition, as the mast surfaces provide an addition to the sail area, the total driving force is further increased. The mast width, however, is not of extreme dimensions and so does not introduce windage

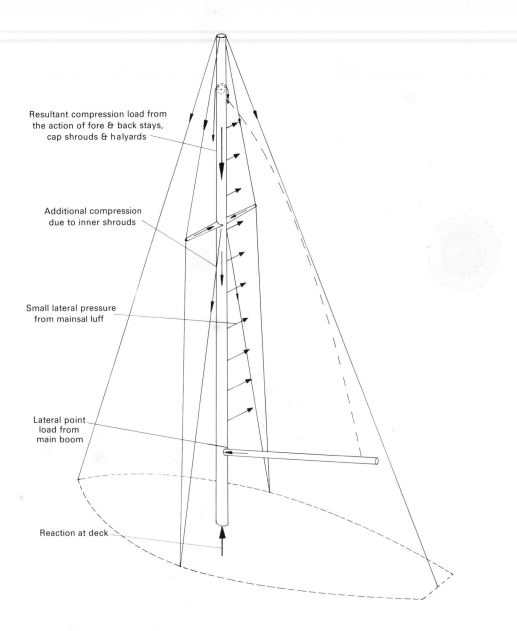

Resultant compression load from
the action of fore & back stays,
cap shrouds & halyards

Additional compression
due to inner shrouds

Small lateral pressure
from mainsal luff

Lateral point
load from
main boom

Reaction at deck

problems when at anchor, and tends to eliminate the disadvantage of sail/mast misalignment found with wing masts. A feature of tri-spar design is that an increase in the span of the side members tends to reduce the slenderness ratio of the material of the mast, permitting higher-designed stresses.

An initial mast was made from mild steel and proved not only the functional aspects, but was also both faster and closer-winded than another dinghy similarly rigged (with mainsail only), even when subjected to a weight handicap of some 100 lb. Subsequently, a prototype was produced in aluminium which demonstrated again its close-winded capabilities, and its speed potential in a 14-ft

'free design' class of dinghy. When used in a current design of boat, the mast was able to beat an Olympic silver medallist to the windward mark. The significance of this performance is that this was the first time the boat had sailed with the rig and there had been no attempt to tune it. Initial trials indicate that with more effort concentrated on the construction design, the sailing qualities of this type of mast would far outstrip those of the traditional extruded section resulting in a mast 30 per cent stronger with a decrease in weight of 20 per cent.

The main problem in production is that it is labour intensive. The prototype was bolted together with hundreds of small nuts and bolts, taking

Fig. 5.1 (*left*). Diagram of the main loads on a mast. In simplified mast design (based on Euler's formula) the smaller lateral loads are ignored and the spar is designed to withstand the large compressive load, resulting from the cap shrouds, forestay and backstay.

Plate 11. The tri-spar: the end-on view (*left*) shows the relatively low-sectioned area subtended to head winds. Sufficient transverse inertia and modulus is obtained from the outer vertical struts. *Photo:* Coles

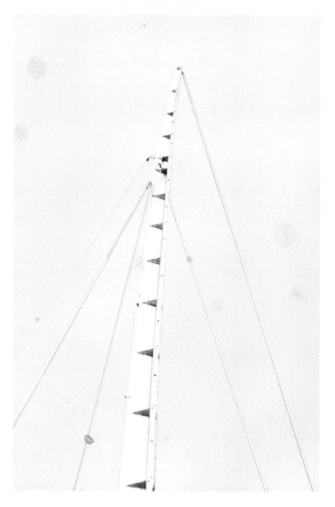

considerable time. Production time could be cut down to a quarter by spot-welding the triangular sections and lattice to the uprights. However, this would still not be as quick a production as the conventional extruded spar section.

Returning to Euler's formula, the compressive load which can be supported by the mast is in direct proportion to the modulus of elasticity of the material used. When investigating the effect of

building spars out of different materials, their moduli and densities must be considered. The three types of mast material of most interest for the future are light alloys, stainless steels and reinforced plastics; Table 5.1 gives their physical and mechanical properties.

Stainless steel has three times the modulus of the suitable light alloys, but its density is approximately three times that of the latter. From the production

Table 5.1. A comparison of properties of mast construction materials

Property	Aluminium alloy	Stainless steel $\frac{1}{4}$ hard	GRP 55% glass content
Density lb/in³	0·098	0·28	0·060
Tensile strength × 10³ lb/in²	40	125	45
Compressive strength × 10³ lb/in²	38 (yield)	67 (yield)	18
Young's modulus × 10⁶ lb/in²	10·3	28	2·2
Specific strength × 10³ lb/in²	14·7	16·0	26·9
Specific modulus × 10⁶ lb/in²	3·8	3·6	1·3

These figures should be read in conjunction with the diagram on the mast sections using the three materials.

Fig. 5.3. Sections through masts built of different materials. Note that the stainless steel mast provides a reduced windage over the conventional aluminium alloy but with an increase in weight. The sections are based on calculations increase in weight. These sections are based on calculations using Euler's formula for struts in compression.

Fig. 5.2 (*right*). Construction details of a tri-spar in way of gooseneck and at shroud attachments.

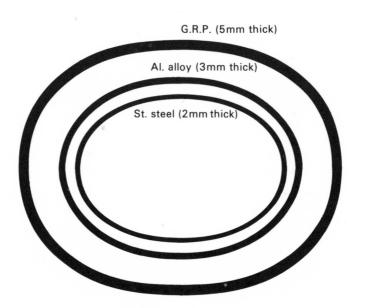

G.R.P. (5mm thick)

Al. alloy (3mm thick)

St. steel (2mm thick)

Ratio Areas and Weights

	Al. Alloy	St. Steel	GRP
X sectional area	108 mm²	61 mm²	264 mm²
Weight	1	1·6	1·5

point of view, there is a minimum thickness of which the mast can be built, but it is still feasible for a far more efficient conventional type of spar to be produced in stainless steel. This would be very costly on a one-off basis, but for racing yachts where performance to windward is a prime consideration, a stainless-steel spar could be tried. The weight penalty would be more than outweighed by the decrease in section. A racing-yacht owner attempting to do well in a race series such as the Admiral's Cup, should consider the great advantage of experimenting with such a spar. Already considerable sums are spent on sails and rigs which produce only slight improvements in performance.

Taking the plunge into something more revolutionary, such as a mast of an unconventional material, might prove to be far more cost-effective in the long run. A comparison of mast sections using these different materials is shown using Euler's formula as the main basis of comparison for a given load (Fig. 5.3).

The wing mast is one of the most interesting developments in the attempt to achieve aerodynamic lift from the compression member. Various types have been tried and are used on some racing classes such as the C Class catamaran. It is clear that with this mast the rig should be fully rotating. At present, wing masts have been used only on relatively small

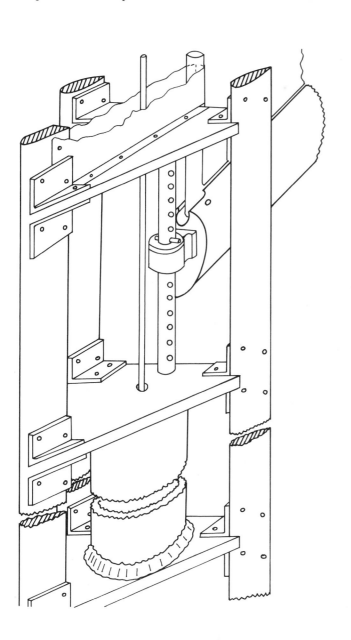

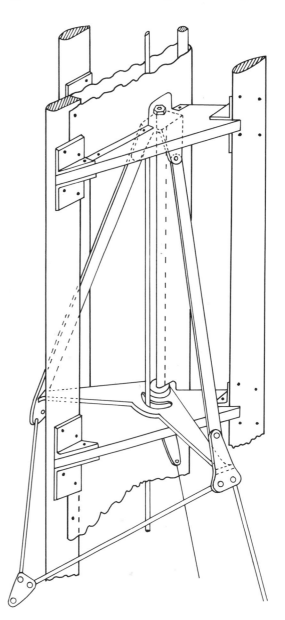

Plate 12. *Lady Helmsman*, a C Class catamaran with fully battened mainsail and wing mast. Note in (*b*) the fine airfoil section and absence of twist in the sail. A highly efficient rig. *Photos:* Farrar of Seahorse Sails Ltd

craft due to the problem of transverse stability and support. For a very tall wing mast, spreaders will have to be fitted if the mast thickness is not to become excessive. A solution to this problem is shown in Fig. 5.4 which uses several diamonds to give the transverse stability enabling the sail and wing to rotate fully about a ball race at the masthead and heel. The mast should rotate quite freely without sails set, so it will present a large windage from the side. This is particularly important when the yacht is moored. The construction of this mast consists of four vertical compression members tied similarly to that of the tripod mast (Fig. 5.2), clad in GRP sheets, weighing as little as 300 g per sq m. These sheets are detachable from the main framework allowing rapid replacement if damaged.

Another interesting development, perhaps more conventional in outlook, is the aluminium extruded

Fig. 5.4. A modern wing mast with fully battened Bermudian sail. In order to achieve the required transverse stability a system of diamond shrouds is adopted with pivots at the mast head and heel to permit full rotation.

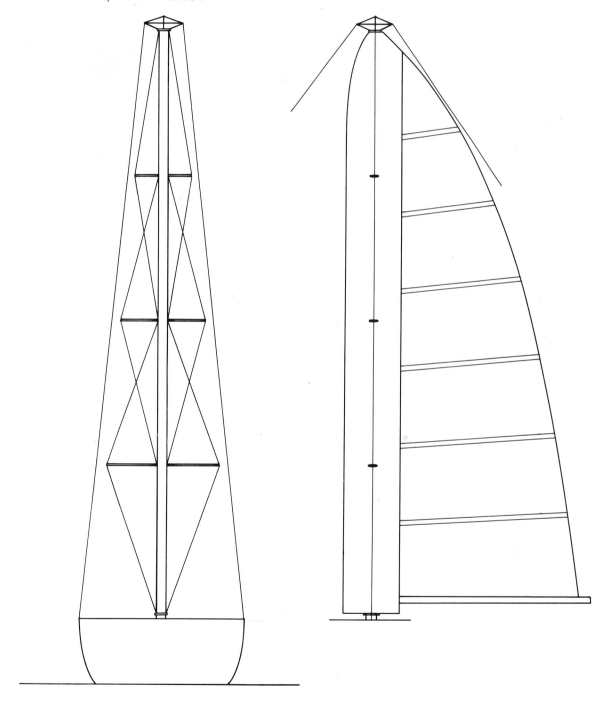

Fig. 5.5. Section through a twin-track alloy mast. The battens run in a slot in the trailing edge of the mast. The build-up of extrusions in way of the tracks increases the inertia about the X-X axis providing greater transverse strength and stability.

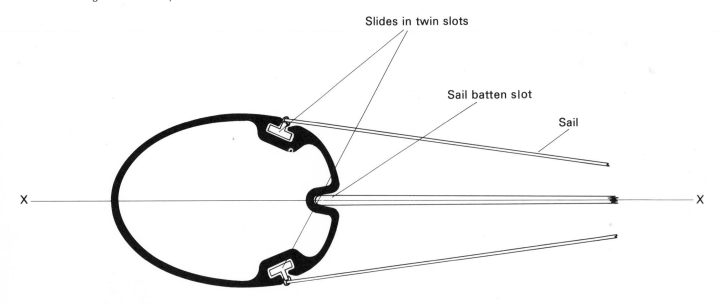

mast with twin tracks down the side (Fig. 5.5). This section has the following advantages: (a) with the extra mass of material in way of the tracks the inertia about the X/X axis is greatly increased, thus the lateral stiffness is also improved, a property which all mast designers are seeking; (b) the sail runs from these tracks in a double-luff arrangement enabling a good aerofoil shape to be achieved on all points of sailing. The mast is fully rotating with a multi-diamond shroud arrangement.

The expected lift from the twin side-track mast, provided twist is properly controlled, is 40 per cent greater than from a conventional rig of the same area. The necessity for mast rotation if any type of aerofoil section is adopted, is demonstrated in Fig. 5.6. A much smaller turbulent area is left behind the mast, provided the major axis is in the direction of the airflow. However, as the airflow becomes tangential to the major axis, this disturbed area is

drastically increased. The circular-section mast is the optimum achieved under conventional design for all angles of attack, but it is a very poor substitute for the aerodynamically-shaped rig.

Masts of present design, although submitting a reasonable section to the wind in windward work, become far less efficient when off the wind. The proposed rig would be superior on all points of sailing.

When the Bermudian mainsail was introduced, exponents of the gaff rig said that the Bermudian rig was inefficient when well reefed due to the large amount of non-useful spar above the headboard, only serving to heel the boat and produce large windage. This is true, for if we consider the amount of mast having no use for a given reduction of area for both the Bermudian and gaff rig, it will be seen from Fig. 5.7 that the high-aspect Bermudian rig is comparatively poor. It is agreed, however, that for

Fig. 5.6. Air disturbance behind elliptical and circular mast sections under beating and reaching conditions. It can be seen that the circular spar gives the greater all-round efficiency.

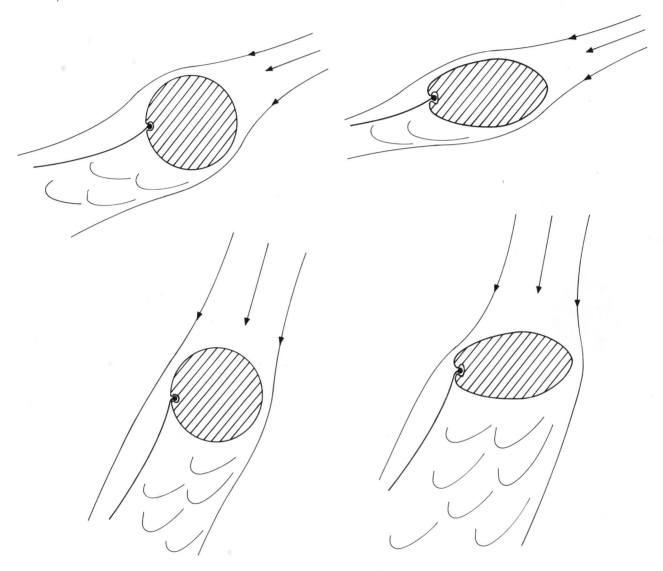

windward work the Bermudian rig is far superior to the standard gaff rig. A telescopic mast is technically feasible for smaller boats, but could also be considered for large offshore racing boats. If the ordinary oval type of mast section is considered, the mast is best reduced from the bottom upwards. The stress on the lower third of the mast is less, by a considerable amount, than that of the peak stress which occurs approximately two-thirds of the way up the mast, and it is possible to collapse the lower third into the thicker upper mast. This would be done by running the shrouds on to winch drums inside the

Fig. 5.7. A comparison of the gaff and Bermudian mainsails when reefed. Note that the gaff is lower by only 60 per cent of the distance by which the Bermudian sail is lowered for an equal reduction in area.

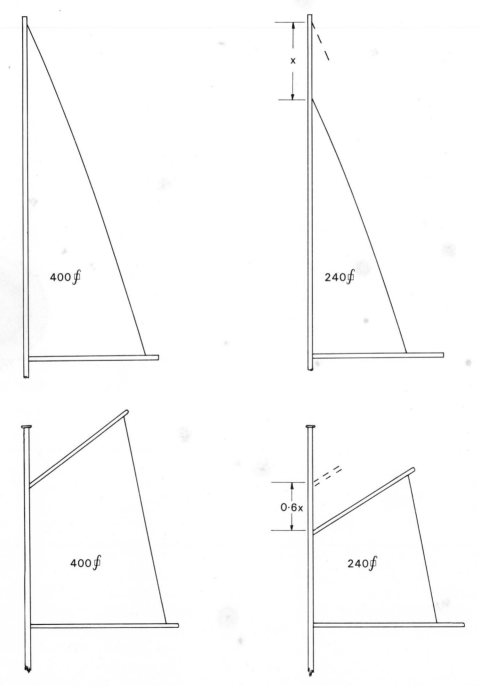

boat, keeping tension on the rigging as required. The lower section of mainsail is held to the mast via a luff wire clipped at various points, thus imposing no restrictions as the lower tube moves inside the upper. Although technically fairly complex and expensive, it produces a rig far more efficient for heavy-weather work, and allows much higher-aspect rigs to be used for light weather than are considered prudent at present.

The biggest development in modern sail production has been the introduction of synthetic fibres. Dacron and Terylene sails are much stronger for a given weight of material, enabling the bias to be controlled with a greater degree of accuracy. Fig. 5.8 and Table 5.2 show the typical weights of sailcloth used for various wind strengths. The light-weather mainsail is included for although it is not usual practice to change the mainsail for varying conditions, if a quick and easy system is adopted such as twin tracks on the trailing edge of the mast, then advantage could be gained while racing. The light main is cut with more camber than the flatter medium-to-heavy sail for although sail shape can be altered with the use of foot outhauls, leech lines and the Cunningham hole, a better shape can be achieved by having the necessary camber already cut into the sail. With development in sailcloths it will be possible to reduce material weights and improve the sailcloth surface to cut down fractional drag.

The weaves of Dacron and Terylene sailcloths have steadily become tighter over the years, further increasing the strength for a given weight and decreasing the porosity of the cloth. If this development is taken to the extreme a plastic produced in sheet form, perhaps with the molecules running in specific directions, would produce an even better material. The direction of least bias, or stretch of cloth, would be in line with the orientation of these molecules. Curvature could be put into the material by welding together panels similarly to the way in which sails are at present made up. The welding might be carried out quickly and accurately either using ultrasonic vibrational energy or a portable laser beam. An all-polythene type of

Table 5.2. Sail properties (see Fig. 5.8).

Sail	Area (sq ft)	Max. Beaufort No.	Windspeed (knots)	Wind pressure (lb/sq in)	Total load on sail (lb)	Sailcloth weight (oz/sq yd)
Main light	250	3	10	0·40	100	5
Main heavy	250	6 unreefed	27	2·91	728	8
No 1 Genoa (light)	450	3	10	0·40	180	4
No 2 Genoa (heavy)	375	5	21	1·76	660	7
No 1 Jib	250	6	27	2·91	728	7
No 2 Jib	200	7	33	4·35	870	8
No 3 Jib	150	8	40	6·40	960	9
Storm jib	75	above 8	50	10·00	750	10
Trysail	100	above 9	60	14·39	1439	14

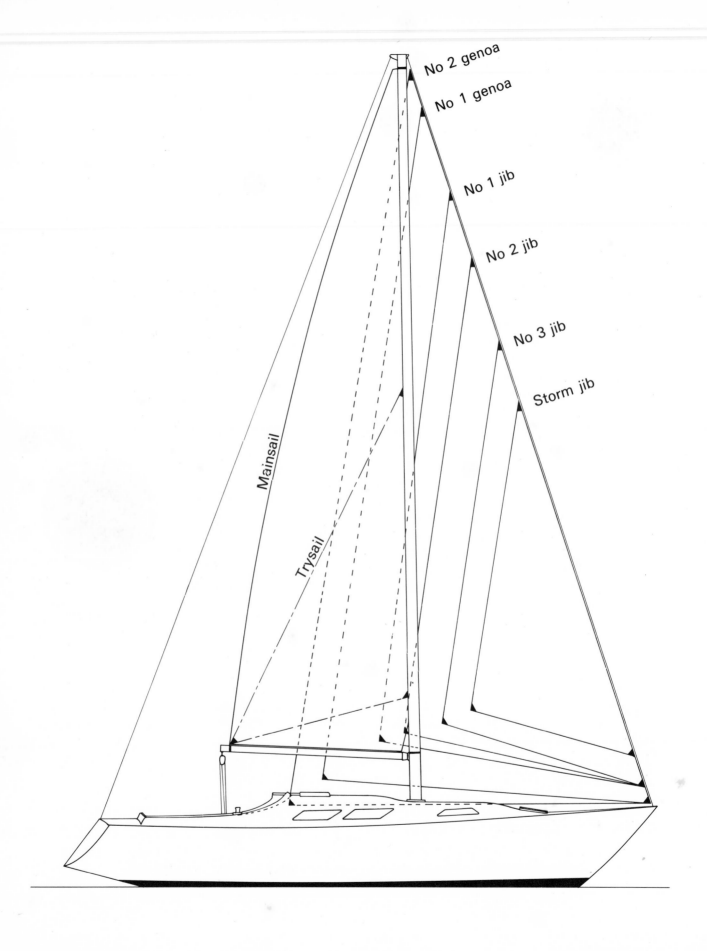

Fig. 5.8 (*left*). Typical headsail arrangement for a modern ocean racing yacht of approximately Three Quarter Ton class. The column in Table 5.2 showing total load on the sail is for a wind normal to the plane of the sail.

Plate 13. A typical wind tunnel model on rotating base for measuring the efficiency of rig at all angles to the wind. This model was used to test a rig for a C Class catamaran.
Photo: Farrar of Seahorse Sails Ltd

mainsail has been tried with the seams welded together, but this material is not suitable as it tends to stretch considerably under strain without very definite bias; in addition a small tear rapidly rips from one end of the sail to the other. If a plastic were produced with molecules running longitudinally and transversely across the material, it would have properties very similar to that of conventional Dacron or Terylene, i.e. with maximum bias at 45° to the weft and warp.

At present little effort is given to controlling sail shape such as using full-length battens and leech outhauls, possibly largely due to the restrictive effect of the off-shore rating rule. However, certain dinghy classes are far ahead in sail control development. The first basis for accurate sail control is the introduction of some transverse stiffening members: the fully battened rig is far more efficient in giving high lift in all wind strengths, as an aerofoil section is held in the material due to the stiffness of these battens. A more efficient rig may be achieved by control of the sail camber and position of maximum draught in the sail by use of batten tension lines and leech lines. A suitable arrangement is shown in Fig. 5.9. This sail enables more camber with maximum draught further aft to be produced for very light wind conditions, or conversely a flat sail for heavy weather.

A fully battened sail with hinged battens enables a flap to be pivoted along the leech. This acts as a lift tab similar to the flaps of aeroplane wings. In high wind strengths, particularly gusty conditions, the flap is slacked off or feathered in the direction of the wind, thus reducing the effective sail area. In light winds the flap is operated in the opposite direction to give a deep camber to the sail. An arrangement using the fully battened mainsail with the double luff mast greatly increases the sailing potential of any type of boat on all points of the wind. It can be seen from

Fig. 5.9 that the battens run up the aft edge of the mast inside a slot, helping to give a continuous fair curve from the mast through to the sail.

An important feature in giving high lift from the Bermudian mainsail is the control and elimination of twist. This has been realised for some time in sailing dinghies, and twist has been prevented by use of a kicking strap or vang. This idea has been adopted on

Fig. 5.9. Fully battened mainsail. Not only is this more efficient due to the control of camber for varying wind conditions, but the battens also permit a greater area to be carried at the head of the sail where the wind speed is greater.

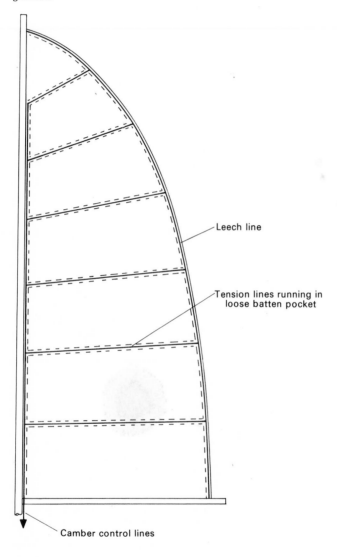

Leech line

Tension lines running in loose batten pocket

Camber control lines

offshore racing boats and today the lift produced by the mainsail of a given area on a fine reach is much higher by virtue of this twist control. The importance of twist control is shown in Fig. 5.10. It can be seen that typical twist exhibited by the

Bermudian mainsail without a kicking strap or vang increases drag when reaching by as much as 20 per cent.

The upper part of a Bermudian mainsail is extremely inefficient for windward work, as a disproportionately large mast is immediately in front of a small length of sail which, due to twist, has fallen off in the lee of the mast (Fig. 5.11). Dinghies such as the Merlin Rockets have reduced this narrow, inefficient area of sail by using a long top batten. The inefficiency can be overcome on large craft to some extent by using a wishbone arrangement for the quadrilateral mainsail, such as was used successfully by *Pen Duick III*. More complete sail control can be carried out by using a modern form of gaff rig with bending spars for both the gaff and main boom. The twist is controlled by kicking straps on the boom running in a semi-circular track across the deck, with a control wire running from the peak of the gaff to the deck edge. This vang is set up with the yacht going to windward or fine-reaching so that the gaff runs in line with the boom. This, in conjunction with the controllable fully-battened sail, permits complete control of camber and the elimination of all twist in the sail. For a given sail area the windward performance of such a rig would greatly exceed that of the conventional Bermudian offshore rig. In addition, offwind, or running, the vertical centre of effort in a sail is lower than that of the Bermudian rig for a given area. These sails would produce much greater power for a given angle of heel, permitting planing possibilities for offshore yachts.

The Bermudian mainsail is ineffective at the top due not only to the detrimental effects of the mast and twist, but also to the air from the high-pressure side which travels across the top of the sail to the low-pressure side, drastically decreasing lift. This can be controlled in the gaff or gunter rig by the

Fig. 5.10. The driving force against drag for twisted and untwisted Bermudian mainsails. It can be seen that the typical twist exhibited by the Bermudian main without a kicking strap increases drag by as much as 20 per cent.

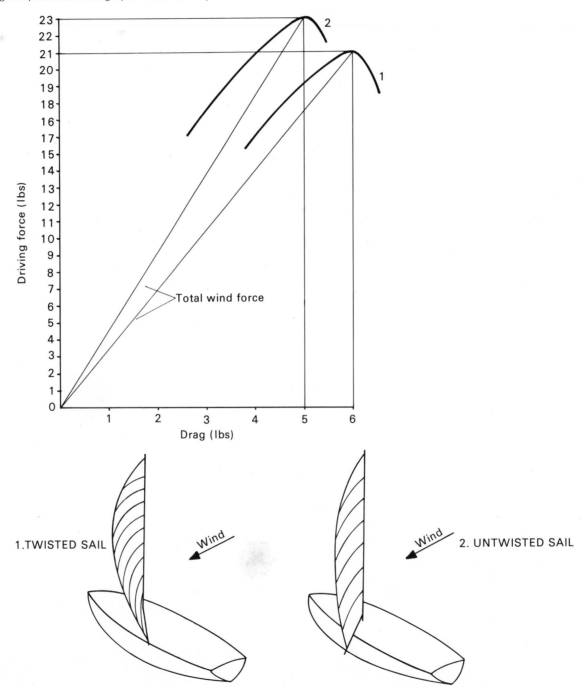

Fig. 5.11. Sections of typical Bermudian mainsail behind mast. It can be seen that twist results in low efficiency at the head of the sail, while at the foot the angle of attack is too severe resulting in excessive drag. The area of optimum efficiency is concentrated towards the centre of the sail.

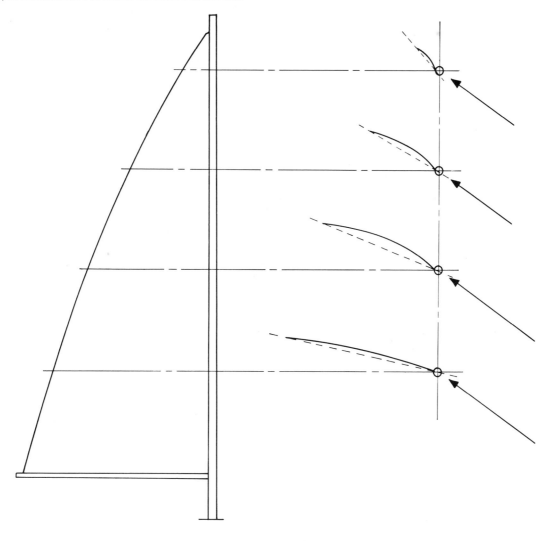

flow-stopping effect of the spar at the head of the sail. Attempts have been made to introduce barriers to airflow from one side to the other along the sail foot. *Enterprise*'s wide, flat 'Park Avenue boom' (as it was nicknamed) with slides across the boom, to allow strict camber setting along the foot of the sail and prevent airflow around the boom, was an attempt to improve mainsail characteristics. However, the need for airflow preventers from one side of the sail to the other is far less necessary along the foot as the airflow patterns tend to run towards the head of the sail as the yacht heels, and the 'Park Avenue' boom, apart from being heavy to control, had the disadvantage that when the yacht was heeled

extensively it disturbed the airflow along the base of the main.

For the large offshore cruising or charter yacht having a limited crew, the high-cut quadrilateral foresail has many advantages. It permits efficient lift to be developed along its full length for the area set. In the case of the cutter rig, tacking may be more easily carried out as there is not the large area of cloth in way of the clew to fold around the inner forestay when going about (Fig. 5.12). The main disadvantage of this sail is that to set up the correct tension at both clews is often difficult, resulting in creases. This problem can be reduced by running two sheets to a single part at the winch. The quadrilateral jib having a clew high up the leech has

a particular advantage when set with the modern gaff rig, as a correct overlap can be achieved over the full length of both sails. The uppermost sheet is led to a swivel block mounted on the transom, or as far aft as is practicable.

Flush-decked yachts of heavy camber, even as short as 30 ft, are fashionable at present. Their arrangement is good aerodynamically, provided the boom is kept low and, with no coachroof preventing ready access to the mainsail, they are far easier for the crew to work. However, care has to be exercised when going forward under severe conditions, for grabrails on the side of a coachroof are safer than crawling along on hands and knees on a flush deck. The deck arrangement lends itself to the loose-footed

Fig. 5.12. The quadrilateral foresail with a gaff main. The quadrilateral sail enables tacking to be more easily carried out as there is not the large area of cloth in way of the clew to fold around the inner stay when going about. Also a greater area of cloth is distributed towards the head of the sail where the wind speeds are greater.

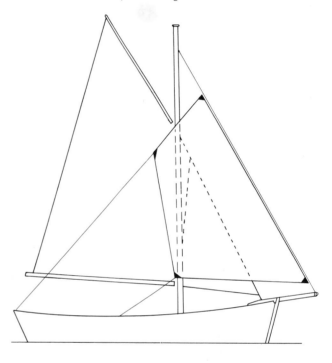

mainsail. An interesting development in mainsail design is to dispense with the boom for windward work, and run a curved track in way of the mainsail clew, so that the foot of the sail touches the flush deck along its length. The sail runs between stops in the track when tacking, and for off-wind work a boom is fastened to an eye in the mast and one at the clew, similar to the arrangement used for spinnakers. Thus the sail forms a continuation of the hull, so that the low pressure along the lee side of the foot is not increased by air flowing underneath from windward. It permits quick changes of mainsail according to wind conditions, so that a light sail cut very full can be used under light conditions, or a heavier, lower-aspect, flatter sail can be set in strong winds. If a double track is run up the trailing edge of the mast it is possible to lose no speed when changing sail as the second main can be hoisted while the first is still set.

A further development in boom design is the adoption of a deck gooseneck fitting with a track running across the full width of the deck. This increases the effective length of the boom for off-wind work by half the beam of the boat, permitting a larger, longer-footed mainsail to be set under light conditions. It also allows small yachts such as Quarter Tonners a method of reefing the mainsail by rotating the mast and rolling the sail about the mast section where, with careful design, spreaders are eliminated.

The IOR rule has encouraged the use of large headsails, sometimes 180 per cent of the mainsail. A large overlap tends to be inefficient for the area of sail used, as often a large proportion of the mainsail is backwinded during windward work. If large headsails continue to be encouraged by the rating rules, it will be desirable to cut away the forward lower part of the mainsail at the tack as shown in Fig. 5.13. The area removed is that which is

normally backwinded, and is anyway of an inefficient shape if the sail is made full enough for a foot zipper to be sewn into it. Cutting this area away will reduce the effective sail area and thus an allowance on rating might well be given, although no difference in speed of windward work should result.

A further anomaly encouraged by the offshore rating rule is that a $\frac{7}{8}$ rig is permitted a greater sail area than masthead rig, although if of equal area these two rigs will show virtually no difference in performance. The $\frac{7}{8}$ rig, although lacking an overlap at the top of the mast, is compensated by the mast section at the top which may be much thinner than that of the masthead rig, as the compression load is considerably reduced on this section. This leads to a reduced blocking effect on the mainsail behind the upper mast. However, for off-wind work, the

Fig. 5.13. Cut-away section of mainsail in way of headsail overlap which is normally inefficient due to back-winding from the fore-triangle.

Plate 16 (*right*). *Vendredi Treize* at the start of the Single-handed Transatlantic Race. This unusual rig, though easy to handle, is not very efficient, as the large gap between sails results in a poor 'slot effect'. The leading edge of the sail, however, is more effective as there is not the large mass of mast in front of this important region of sail. *Photo:* Beken

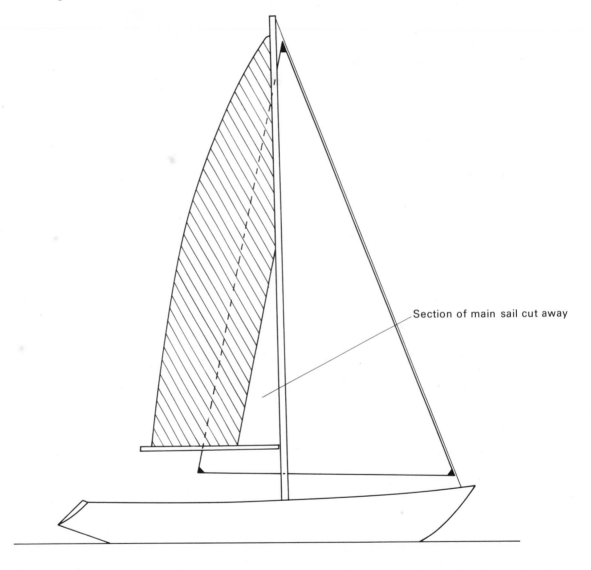

Section of main sail cut away

spinnaker will be carried lower down and thus is less efficient and of smaller area. If sail efficiency and ease of handling are of prime consideration, the rating rule should be ignored and the most efficient rig for the number of crew available to work it should be developed.

There should be far more co-operation between sail and mast designers in order to increase efficiency at the masthead. Fig. 5.14 shows the increase in wind strengths for height above the surface of the sea for varying sea-level wind conditions. It will be appreciated that the top of the

sail is important regarding performance, particularly under light wind conditions, as this is where a high driving force can be achieved. This part of the sail is free also from interference from airflow patterns caused by the hull. If rig designers devoted their efforts to twist control and camber variation at this section, sailing-yacht performance would be considerably improved for windward work.

For the larger racing yacht a good approximate guide is that one man cannot handle more than 400 sq ft of sail. This assumes that the yacht will sometimes be caught with too much sail in bad sea conditions, when working is most difficult. The owner of a yacht of 60 ft or over, particularly if he

does not wish to race under the IOR rule, should carefully consider the advantages of the schooner rig with masts of approximately equal size. This rig is particularly useful with limited crew as the sail areas can be split into the maximum which can be handled easily by two men (Fig. 5.15). The drawings show that a wide variation of sail can be adopted according to prevailing conditions. If the mainsail and foresail are of equal size, these sails can be interchanged if one becomes damaged, so that the yacht can be balanced properly.

Much time and head-scratching have been put into mast and rigging development so that a tight, straight forestay can be set up on ocean racers. This

Modern development in yacht design

Fig. 5.14. Variation in wind speed at different heights above
sea level. It can be seen that below 10 ft the wind speed
starts to decrease rapidly.

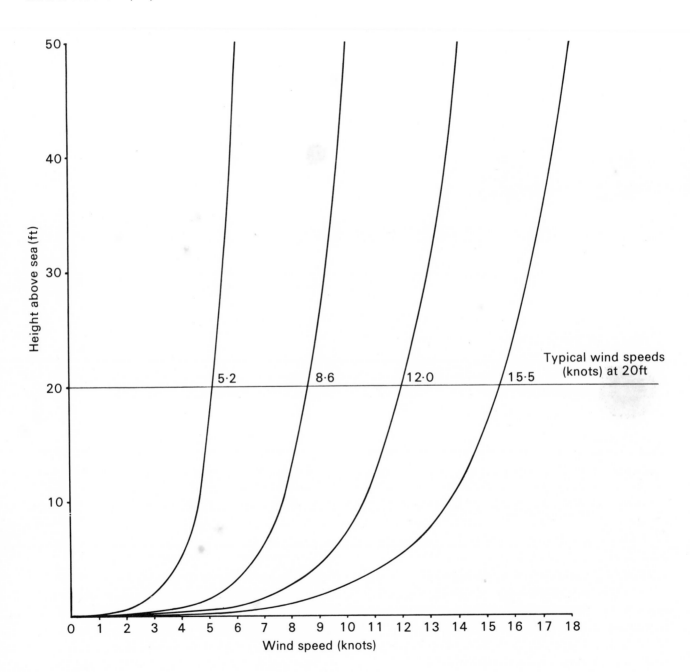

Plate 17. *Planesail P1* leaping windward in a short chop off Chichester, England. The four vertical wingmasts can rotate through 360° and the direction vane aft is counterbalanced by the weight forward. All the controls are handled from the forward, aircraft-type cockpit. *Photo:* Anthony Linton by courtesy of Planesail Ltd

is indeed very necessary as the headsail luff will tend to sag to leeward and the boat will not point up properly if insufficient tension is put into the forestay. Hydraulic backstays have enabled very high tensions to be set up in the fore and aft rigging, to such an extent that in some GRP yachts, particularly those with shallow hull sections as are found on many of the latest fin and skeg arrangements, the hull itself has been bent due to the high compression load from the mast near the centre. This can be observed when the backstay is being set up, as the guard rails may be found to slacken. The search for a straight luff has led to the introduction of rod rigging incorporating a groove

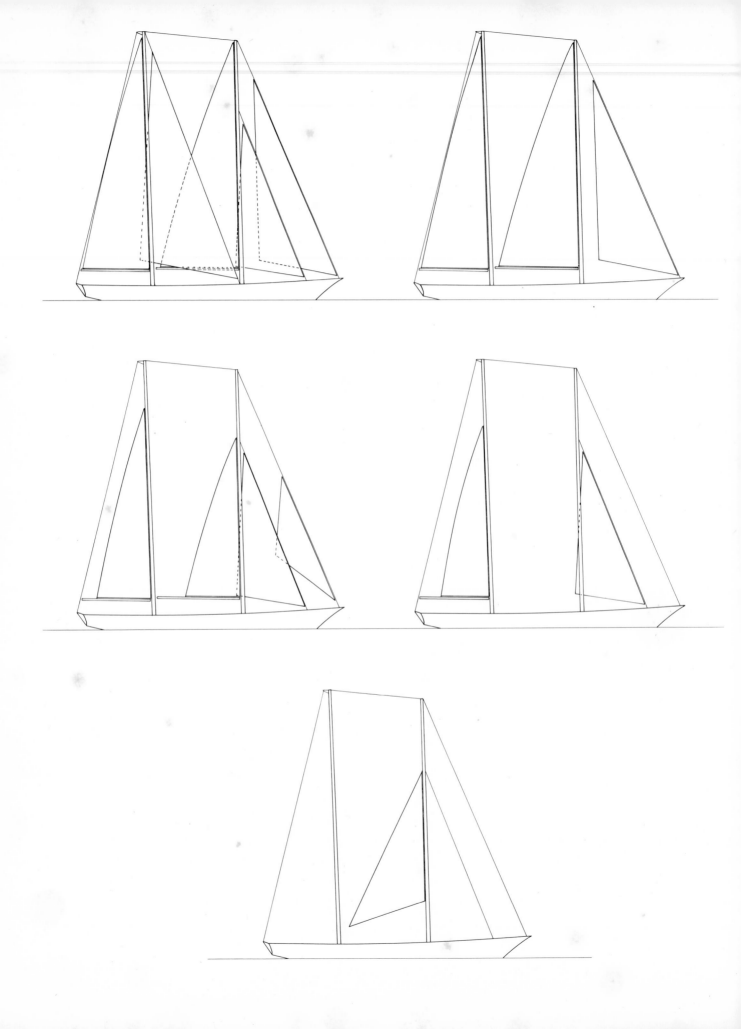

Fig. 5.15 (*left*). Sail combinations for modern schooner rig showing how sail area may be reduced with increasing wind strength but maintaining correct sail balance.

Fig. 5.16. A comparison between the pressure distribution on a Bermudian and gunter rig. It can be seen that provided twist is eliminated from the gunter rig that this shape is more efficient at the head of the sail where the wind speed is greater.

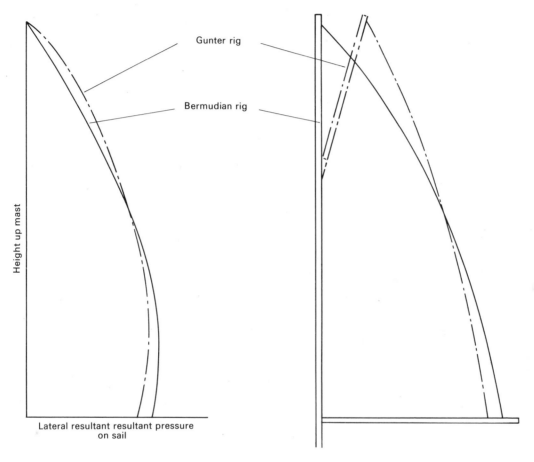

Gunter rig

Bermudian rig

Height up mast

Lateral resultant resultant pressure on sail

for the headsail luff for the jib to run-up similar to that for the mainsail. Rod rigging has the disadvantage that it is more expensive, and is not easily transported or stowed. Great care should be taken to examine the rods at their attachment points at the end of the season as they are prone to fatigue. It might be worth while having the rigging x-rayed after it has been in use for two or three seasons to determine whether any fatigue cracks are present.

The case for a modified gaff rig on the modern offshore racing yacht has already been outlined, where the sail is more efficient at the head and twist reduction effected. The gunter rig also has many interesting advantages, particularly with the development of synthetic fibre sails and alloy spars. This rig permits a narrower spar to be fitted to the upper two-thirds of the mainsail, thus increasing the effectiveness of the sail behind the spar. Also, in a similar fashion to the gaff rig, a vang can be run from the peak of the main to the windward side aft to minimise twist, the main disadvantage of this rig for windward work. The rig offers considerable

Fig. 5.17. The fitting of end plates to a modern gunter rig.
These end plates can increase the driving force from the sail
by as much as 15 per cent. Their action is to restrict flow
from the high pressure to the low pressure side at the ends
of the sail.

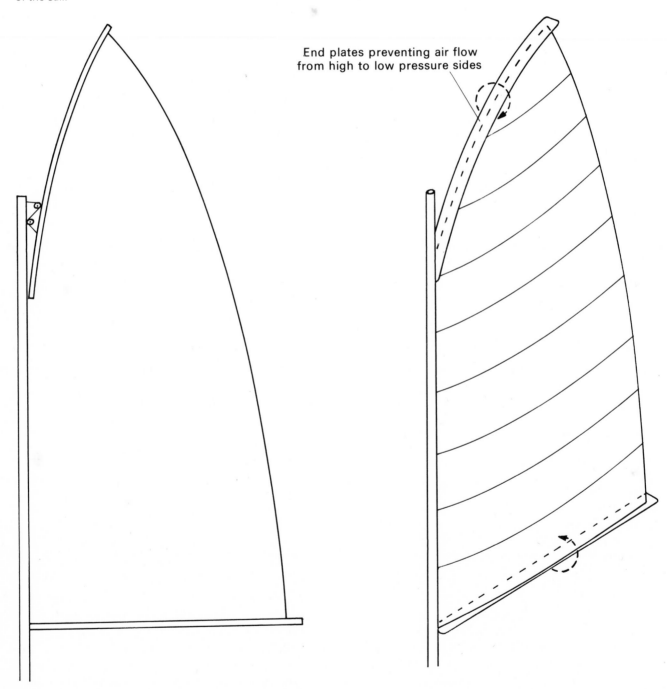

End plates preventing air flow
from high to low pressure sides

Fig. 5.18. The fully battened headsail. Not only do the battens provide a more efficiently controlled camber but also give support to the luff helping to eliminate sag.

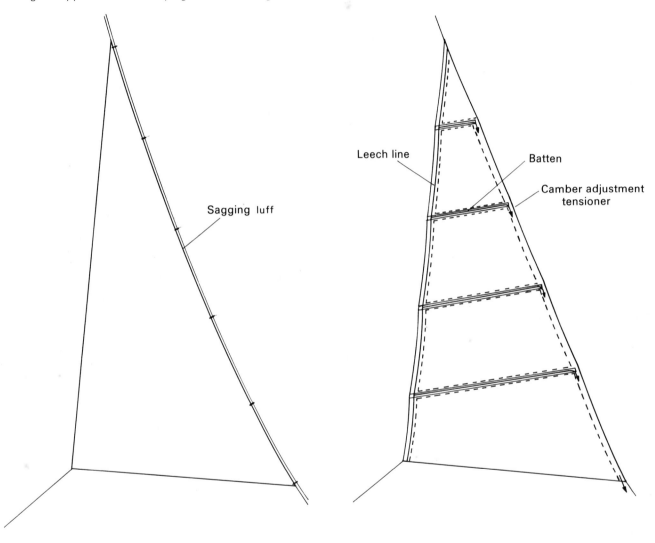

Sagging luff

Leech line

Batten

Camber adjustment tensioner

advantages in heavy weather conditions as the weight of supporting spar when the mainsail is reefed is lower than that of the equivalent Bermudian rig, and may be considered to be equivalent to the telescopic mast. Typical pressure distributions of the gunter and the conventional Bermudian main are shown in Fig. 5.16. A further advantage of the gunter rig is that a higher lift/drag ratio can be achieved at the top of the rig due to the increased wind strengths in this area, provided twist is efficiently controlled. The aerodynamic-section gunter rig can be achieved in a similar method to that used in the twin-track system shown for the Bermudian mainsail (Fig. 5.5). The gunter spar should have a pre-set curve along its length permitting greater sail area to set at the top of the rig, as shown in Fig. 5.17. An end plate can be welded to the top of the leading edge of the spar to help prevent flow from the high- to low-pressure areas across the sail. The only disadvantage is that the jib cannot be set from the head of the mainsail, but, provided the spar at the head is not excessively long, the rig becomes equivalent to the older $\frac{3}{4}$ or $\frac{7}{8}$ rig, with associated rule advantages.

The benefits of the fully battened mainsail mentioned earlier also apply to the foresail, with the additional gain that, if the battens are fitted to the sail so that the leech is tensioned (Fig. 5.18), the sag in the luff may be considerably reduced. Experiments have been carried out on fully-battened jibs both in Britain and the US and have proved the increased efficiency of the sail. The battens permit easier camber control, as in the mainsail but, if the battens are to be fitted under tension to reduce sag, then ideally a boom should be fitted to the foot of the sail.

6

Engines and powering

The usual system of powering yachts today is the internal combustion engine, but its origins have been inherited from a long tradition of marine steam power. It is probable that world oil shortages will force engine development to prepare for a radical change. The future may lie in improved forms of steam powering or the adoption of battery electric power for slower craft.

The development of compact marine steam engines during the nineteenth century reached a peak with the high-speed reciprocating engines designed and built by concerns such as Simpson Strickland & Co., of Dartmouth, England, the Herreshoff Manufacturing Co. of Newport, Rhode Island, John I. Thornycroft & Co., of Chiswick, London, Schichau of Bremen, Normand of Le Havre and many comparable firms building fast launches and large naval torpedo craft. Steam reciprocating machinery in large pleasure craft was displaced eventually by the steam turbine, but in smaller yachts the steam engines after 1900 were challenged increasingly by the internal combustion petrol engine which, despite its initial poor power/weight ratio, grew constantly in popularity because of its compactness and its lack of need of attention when not delivering power. With the simultaneous development of motor road transport the all-important minimum weight and fuel consumption for power constantly improved.

In 1907 the American designer Clinton Crane, with his brother, designed and had constructed a 40-ft racing motor boat *Dixie II* for E. J. Schroeder to defend the Harmsworth International Motor Boat Trophy. The petrol engine weighed 2205 lb and developed 110 h.p. at 20 lb per h.p. This was light enough to 'fly' and indicates the very early realisation of the internal combustion engine's potential. This boat logged just under 37 m.p.h., which the same designer, with *Dixie IV* of 1910, advanced to 47 m.p.h.

In 1914 Atkin Wheeler, yacht designers and builders at Huntingdon, Long Island, designed and built the hull and main engines for the 115-ft motor yacht *Cabrilla*. These V-type 8-cylinder petrol engines weighed 5500 lb each and developed 750 h.p. at 1400 r.p.m. It is of interest to note that the deck was planked with two skins of waterproof plywood of Russian manufacture.

The first recorded aeroplane flight made by the Wright brothers in 1903 was contemporary with the first attempts to increase radically the speed of motor-propelled craft. In 1905 the Wrights' aeroplane succeeded in maintaining 38 m.p.h., and in the same year the best speed in the Gold Cup Race for power boats was made by H. A. Lozier's *Shooting Star* at 24·2 m.p.h. In August 1939 Sir Malcolm Campbell's *Bluebird* was timed at 141·74 m.p.h. and in August 1956, *Slo Mo'shun IV* broke up while holding the world record for a propeller-driven hull at 178·5 m.p.h. Thus over the past 70 years the rapid development of the internal combustion engine has enabled the achievement of these recordbreaking high speeds. It is interesting to note the rapid change in speed of motor yacht development compared with the much slower development of hull form design and rig improvement for sailing boats. The development of power/weight ratios for the internal combustion engine will undoubtedly slow down with more effort being devoted to the development of small low-powered turbines, which will provide a great jump ahead in power/weight ratio and comfort due to the lack of noise and vibration.

Marine Diesels

The most common type of engine favoured in pleasure cruising yachts is the marine diesel. Early diesel engines were slow speed, ranging from between 75 to 500 r.p.m., with higher speeds restricted by contemporary injection systems, combustion chamber design and metallurgical and engineering knowledge. A long stroke was considered essential for efficiency, but this also restricted piston speeds. These engines were large and heavy, air or cartridge starting and direct reversing were essential, and drip-feed lubrication caused high oil consumption. They were initially expensive, but their comparative compactness and running economy were improvements on the steam engine.

During the 1920s improvements in diesel engine fuel-injection systems, materials, lubricating oils and reduction gears encouraged the development of medium-speed engines. This was followed by the use of forced feed lubrication for bearing surfaces, reverse gears and mechanical fuel injection. Development of the automotive diesel engine's greater revolutions and power/weight ratios extended further the use of high-speed engines, and the Second World War proved their reliability. For many years it was held that engines must not have piston speeds in excess of 1500 ft per min to ensure long and reliable service, but high-speed diesels running at speeds of 1700 ft per min and above and giving about one-third longer life between overhauls soon disproved this. Reduction in piston diameter enabled the stroke to be reduced and cylinder numbers increased with consequent permissible increase in r.p.m. while retaining the piston speed of older engines with longer stroke. In some high-speed diesel engines piston stroke is actually shorter than in the old medium- and slow-speed engines, resulting in less frictional loss. Improvements in the design and construction of mechanically operated fuel injection systems have contributed greatly to high-speed diesel development, and most engines of this type now inject at 10,000 to 17,000 p.s.i. pressure.

Although the diesel is a heat engine, temperatures must be kept within a certain range or materials and engine components will rapidly deteriorate: thus engine cooling is most important. The hottest place is of course the combustion chamber, of which the piston crown forms one side. Here high-speed diesels with smaller diameter cylinders have an advantage over medium- or slow-speed engines, due to the shorter distance heat has to travel before reaching the cooling medium, and to improving metallurgical and operational factors. Although oil cooling of pistons is common to all diesels, oil is not so efficient a cooling medium as water and almost all high-speed diesels are now fresh water cooled through a heat exchanger and keel cooling. This allows engines to be run at much higher temperatures than would be possible if sea water, whose salt precipitates, were used directly. It is an advantage for these engines to run at higher temperatures as all the internal working surfaces are thus at a similar temperature and wear is reduced. Cooling systems are now usually thermostatically controlled to ensure a more even temperature regardless of sea and air temperatures, and most high-speed diesels now operate between 165° and 195° F (74° C and 91° C).

Fresh water also allows a pressurised cooling system operating at about 12 p.s.i., raising the boiling point of the water to 225° F (107° C) and above, further reducing wear on moving parts and allowing use of less refined fuels with higher sulphur content.

Development of reliable, hydraulically operated reverse gears has further encouraged use of high-speed diesel engines. The gears have their own complete and independent oiling system, with forced feed lubrication to all bearings and gears, and are compact units, steadily reducing in size. Horsepower loss through gearing, including reduction gears, seldom exceeds 2 per cent of the through b.h.p. However, gearboxes still represent a considerable proportion of the total cost of engine plus gearbox.

High-speed engines have forced-feed lubrication to every part which ensures the supply of the correct quantity of oil to every bearing surface, and the latest diesel development incorporates needle roller bearings on the main bearings. The high-speed engine generally only uses 0·0025 lb of lubricating oil per b.h.p. per hour, but even this small amount can be considerable over long periods of continuous running. The small-diameter pistons of high-speed diesels make it more difficult to obtain complete atomisation of injected fuel and they therefore burn slightly more fuel than those having larger diameter pistons, though all the fuel is burned. The specific fuel consumption of high-speed diesels is around 0·42 lb per b.h.p. per hour.

High-speed diesels are manufactured in great numbers for automotive and other uses, of which the marine market seldom takes more than about 15 per cent of factory production.

Gas Turbines

Race boats are perpetually seeking engines with as high a power/weight ratio as possible, ideally less than 1 lb per h.p. developed. The modern, compact gas turbines, produced by the large motor companies and developing upwards of 150 h.p., are very suitable, but these smaller engines have not yet been tried extensively in the faster power boats. At present, the more successful racing craft tend to use multiple large outboards as these engines, apart from the turbines, give the most beneficial power/weight ratio. Typically, a 100-h.p. outboard weighs about 180 lb. The Rover gas turbine first made its debut when fitted to both saloon and racing cars in the mid 1960s; however, these types were not developed fully in racing cars and several serious accidents occurred during development. The principal problem with this type of engine in automobiles is the delay between pressing the accelerator and achieving power. However, for yacht use this delay is of no consequence.

The small turbines run on low-grade fuels such as paraffin with heavy oils being used by the larger turbines, provided there is sufficient air supply. The fuel is fed from a ring of sprayers and mixes with the compressed air emitted from the compression chambers, resulting in continuous combustion. The resulting high-velocity expanded gases are ducted to the compressor turbine rotors to provide the typical vibration-free continuous power.

The Rover gas turbine, weighing 160 lb, delivers 146 continuous b.h.p. with a maximum of 187 b.h.p. Its dimensions are approximately $1·5 \times 1·5 \times 3$ ft and the compressor turbine runs at 64,000 r.p.m. with gearing providing a takeoff of 5000 r.p.m.

A large gas turbine propulsion system typically comprises:

A free piston gas generator, or numbers of generators.
A gas turbine with a number of ahead wheels or, if necessary, one or two astern wheels.
A reduction gear to each shaft, which may also have reverse gear.
Fresh water and oil pumps for cooling and lubrication of the generators, turbines and reduction gears.
Pumps and heat exchangers for the circulating fresh water and oil.
Air compressors and receivers for starting the generators.
Auxiliary equipment, including pumps for fuel and oil transfer, filters etc.

The free piston gas generator comprises a casing,

Fig. 6.1. Diagrammatic section of a modern gas turbine. The early gas turbines used a conventional piston and cylinder arrangement for the compressor unit.

enclosed at each end, having back-flow valves and containing a cylinder liner with injectors, scavenging and exhaust ports, and casings for the two synchronised connecting rods. The two compression chambers at the end of the generator casing and two free pistons which comprise a working part at the centre, with a small high pressure area and a compression part having larger diameter on the outside, work on an air cushion on the outside and as a compressor on the inside; two connecting rods synchronise the action of the pistons. When the pistons reach the inside dead point, the injected fuel is ignited and the pistons are pushed apart again; thus part of the developed power is accumulated in the air cushion. During this movement apart, air is drawn into the compression chambers and the exhaust ports; then the scavenging ports which are connected with the engine casing filled with air under pressure open and enable the exhaust gases to escape and let scavenging air in. This process is similar to a two-cycle engine with opposite pistons. When the pistons reach the limit of their outward stroke, the air cushions restore the energy they have accumulated and the pistons return to inside dead point. During the return movement the compression pistons force air into the compression chambers, into the inside of the cylinder casing through the valves, and the moving pistons close the scavenging and exhaust ports and compress the air to be used for combustion in the next cycle. The mixture of air and gas which escapes is led to the turbine at temperatures of 840–930° F (450–500° C) and is at a pressure of 50 p.s.i.

Reversing is possible by one or several reverse wheels in the turbine, a reverse gear in the reduction gear, or by a controllable pitch propeller.

The gas generator and gas turbine machinery requires less length of engine room than diesel machinery and has a superior power/weight

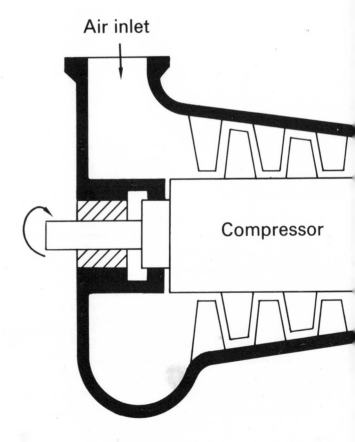

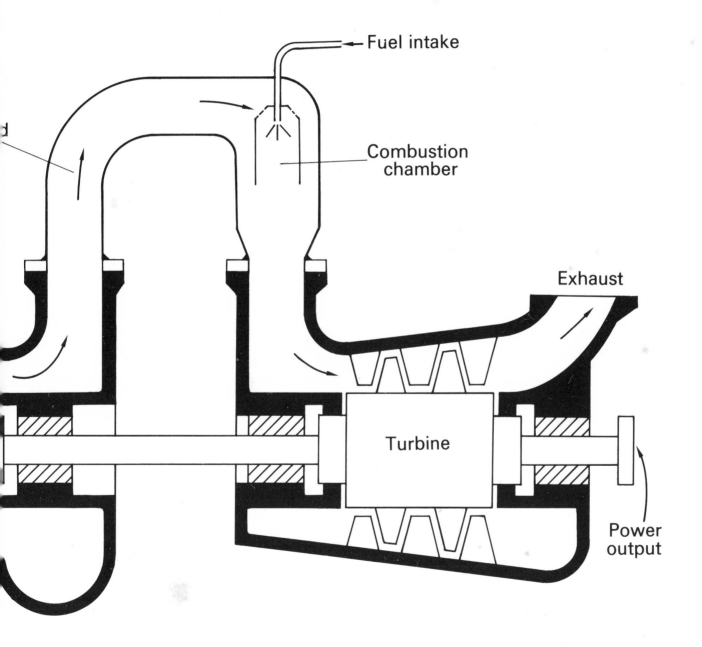

Fuel intake

Combustion
chamber

Exhaust

Turbine

Power
output

ratio compared to diesel engines. Other advantages are:

1. Flexibility of use, as the generators automatically adjust to required changes in power output.
2. Simple reversing with a turbine having a reversing wheel. The generator continues to run while the change is made and the reversing gear wheel instantly takes the impact of the load as it is operating at a temperature of about 580° F.
3. Safety of dividing power between two generators.
4. Comparative ease of dismantling and repair of a generator which can be stripped of movable equipment in about thirty minutes, and replacement of a generator, due to the light weight.
5. Elimination of engine vibration due to the balancing of moving parts; an especially desirable feature in yachts.
6. The generators may be run on heavy fuel because of the excess of air available.

Gas turbine propulsion will be used increasingly in large motor yachts and a typical installation for a 170-ft craft would be two free-piston gas generators developing a total of 1800 h.p. at continuous rating and 2200 h.p. if supercharged. These supply one turbine which drives the shaft, or two shafts, through a reduction gear. The small turbines adopt a rotor compressor instead of the piston type (Fig. 6.1).

Steam Engines

Much interest has been shown during the past few years in the steam engine. Marine steam engines were in fairly widespread use in Britain, Europe and North America much earlier in the nineteenth century than is often realised. Several steam yachts were built by the 1840s, their owners regarded

contemptuously by sailing contemporaries; however, they increased significantly in numbers when the screw propeller was demonstrated as practicable, allowing vessels to be built without disfiguring paddle boxes. The early engines in small vessels, commercial or yacht, were often of experimental design, but the compound engine was popular in Britain until small triple expansion sets were developed in the late 1880s.

In 1885 Yarrow & Co. built torpedo boat No. 79 with triple expansion engines instead of the compound type previously used in high-speed boats. In compound steam engines, steam is led from the boiler to a high-pressure cylinder and, having done some work in that cylinder, it is passed into a second cylinder to complete its usefulness before being exhausted into a condenser. The triple expansion engine uses steam in three stages, passing into the condenser. The principal advantage of the triple over the compound is the greater range of expansion which may be used.

The earlier high-speed steam engines before the middle 1870s suffered from excessive vibration. These types had valves between the cylinders and were very long, and although the whole mass of moving parts could be counter-balanced, the ends of these engines gyrated considerably around the centre of weight. It was partially on account of this vibration trouble of the reciprocating engine that turbine development proceeded. The Herreshoff Manufacturing Company in the early 1870s developed steam engines which were almost completely balanced both statically and dynamically. These engines were 4-cylinder triple expansion with two of the cylinders above, so that together with its valves and valve gear the length of this type was less than half that of most other types of the time. They weighed 18,750 lb and developed 1700 h.p. and ran for twenty years in naval service

Fig. 6.2. Diagrammatic section of a marine jet unit.

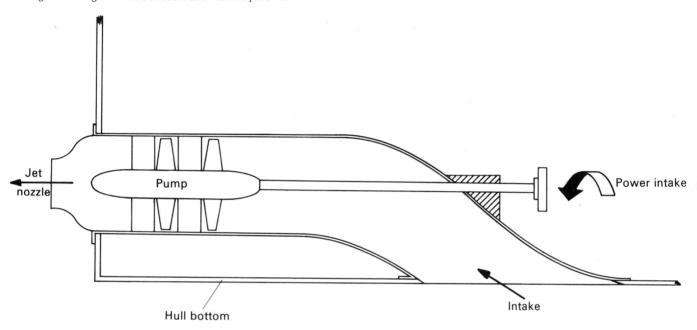

without major overhaul. The boilers of this type were first developed by Captain Du Temple, who had spent most of his life trying to develop a steam-driven flying machine. His boilers brought out in 1873 were the first of the express type from which the Thornycroft, Yarrow, Normand and Herreshoff types descended.

The major disadvantage of these early steam engines was the very high weight of the machinery and the huge reserve of coal that had to be carried aboard to give the craft reasonable steaming distance. For instance, some torpedo boats of the 1880s displaced approximately 190 tons fully loaded of which 76 tons was propelling machinery, and 60 tons of coal was carried for full range. Steam engines will gain popularity in the future, mainly through nostalgia but partly from economic and pollution considerations. These modern types will be

of multiple expansion arrangement and, except in the case of traditional reproductions, will be oil fired. This will have the advantage of automatic feed and a far less displacement requirement placed on the craft. The boilers will be produced from high-tensile aluminium alloys giving excellent heat conduction for very low boiler weight, giving a far greater heating area efficiency than in the earlier types and also permitting very high-pressure superheated steam to be produced, greatly increasing the efficiency of the steam engine.

Marine Jets

One of the most useful recent developments in propulsion for pleasure and commercial craft is that of the marine jet unit (Fig. 6.2), which works on

Fig. 6.3. Efficiency of impeller types in a marine jet unit. It can be seen that at approximately 40 knots the sub-cavitating impeller efficiency is falling off rapidly and the super-cavitating type should be adopted.

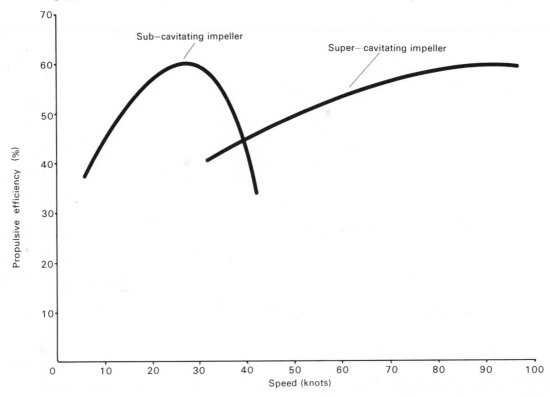

basically the same principle as the normal propeller propulsion except that the propeller blades or pump impeller is mounted inside the craft with inlets usually in the hull bottom. This system has the great advantage that appendage drag may be eliminated as rudders are replaced by the rotation of the jet nozzle. Such craft can operate successfully where perhaps only an inch of water exists under the hull and, provided the hull is made strong enough, this system allows the craft to run over marshland and the like where only a hovercraft could travel in the same way.

For lower speeds the marine jet unit tends to be less efficient than conventional propulsion, but for higher velocity of intake this system becomes more efficient, particularly as appendage drag increases rapidly with speed.

For speeds greater than about 35 knots the conventional propeller undergoes some degree of cavitation, and the transition from non-cavitating to super-cavitating propellers is a critical one; it is during the range of partial cavitation that the propeller blades suffer most erosion, due to the collapse of the water vapour bubbles causing small masses of water to hit the blade surface with great velocity. The marine jet unit usually does not suffer from the same problem as a high-pressure mixture of water and water vapour is produced at the first stage of the impeller and cavitation is completely suppressed. At low speeds cavitation can occur particularly when accelerating as there is a considerable pressure drop at the entrance to the intake duct. This will not normally result in cavitation damage as the craft will quickly accelerate through this stage. The graph (Fig. 6.3) indicates the type of propulsive efficiency for varying speed that would be expected from a marine jet unit. Above 60 knots the unit becomes far more efficient than conventional systems. Up to about 40 knots the sub-cavitating propeller would be adopted and below 40 knots the jet unit is less efficient than conventional drive, but this may be offset to some extent by the advantage of no appendages. This system of drive coupled to the modern low-weight gas turbine would produce an extremely efficient drive system for a very high-speed craft such as a race boat designed to exceed 70 knots.

The trend over the past forty years, particularly accelerated during the last ten years with the advent of the very light displacement motor yacht, has been to increase the shafting angle. This has an adverse effect on thrust and is probably one of the major influencing factors causing modern fast power boats, with all the latest developments in materials, to be only just as fast as their early predecessors. For instance, *Maple Leaf IV* (Chapter 3) achieved 55 knots in 1912 with engines developing 800 h.p. resulting from 9 lb engine weight per horsepower. Modern petrol engines in the 400 h.p. range weigh under 2 lb per horsepower, and yet even with this great weight advantage few of the race boats can beat their predecessors. Undoubtedly the hull form of these race boats was an important influencing factor in their success as is admirably demonstrated by *Lulworth*, designed and built by S. E. Saunders of Cowes in 1920. She attained a speed of 36 knots on a single 275-h.p. engine. With a length overall of 40 ft and a single step in the bottom she displaced 3·68 tons. Of course these craft were not able to maintain

high speeds in the types of sea encountered by the modern power boats when racing, as they tended to have no deadrise aft, causing severe slamming and structural failure.

As few modern diesels can run at over a $15°$ installation angle, resulting in $16–17°$ in planing trim, the V-drive has been developed, giving an effective increased length of shafting enabling the propeller shaft to be installed at minimum rake. The V-drive has the added advantage that the machinery may be installed in the aft end of the yacht, thus reducing noise and vibration in the rest of the accommodation area. The engine room of such a yacht would have both engines and generators as well as all the sterngear sited together, enabling easy access to all the machinery. There are two major problems associated with the modern trend of positioning engines aft: strength, and the location of the longitudinal centre of gravity (LCG). This V-drive type of installation usually means that the engines are supported aft of where the main keel skeg finishes. This has led to serious stress cracking of the steel plating in some larger craft due to the lack of longitudinal rigidity, particularly if any of the engines should be out of balance. The second problem is that of achieving the correct trim under all powering conditions with this large weight aft. The motor yacht incorporating this type of drive has to have a large water-plane area aft to provide sufficient buoyancy for the engines. Craft of this type tend to have wide transoms resulting in high resistance at low speeds, that is up to a $V/\sqrt{L}$ of 1·8; above this speed the large planing area aft gives lift. The 40-ft cruising motor yacht with a maximum speed of 10 knots ideally should not be designed to have this large water-plane area at the transom as it will cause excessive wave-making resistance at these lower speeds: such cruising types should have their engines as near midships as possible and should have a fairly balanced curve of areas similar to the lines plan of the old steam yachts, long and narrow with waterline hollows at each end. The tendency in motor-yacht design to achieve as much accommodation in as short a length as possible has resulted in the wide beam being run right up to the transom for all speed types so there is little problem in positioning the engines, and the V-drive with engines by the transom tends to be preferred.

Another way of overcoming the problem of the steep shafting angle is by the adoption of hydraulic drive. Using this system the engines may be sited anywhere convenient, and as low in the boat as possible, allowing sufficient depth of engine girders to provide adequate strength. Power is transmitted to the propellers by high-pressure piping using hydraulic fluids and the propellers are housed on a vertical pod through the boat's bottom, thus achieving maximum thrust as the shafting angle can be set to zero inclination.

This system has the disadvantage of frictional loss in power from the hydraulic fluid causing approximately 15 per cent power loss. The alternative sometimes used is solid coupling, so that the shafting runs through two right angles via bevel gears to the propeller, again mounted on a pod. Hydraulic drives capable of taking horsepowers greater than about 100 are not yet as reliable as conventional drive, but undoubtedly this type of coupling will be developed in the future enabling it to be used in very large motor yachts or high-speed race boats.

An interesting arrangement enabling ease of access to engines as well as sufficient cool air to be supplied to the intakes would be to mount the engines on the deck aft with the accommodation underneath, the power being delivered to the props by hydraulic drive. This arrangement could be most suitably used in canal and lake cruisers where stability under severe sea conditions is of no importance.

For the large motor yacht using hydraulic drive, bow propellers on a rotating pod may be run off the main engine. In harbours and confined waters, where manoeuvring becomes difficult, the bow propeller can be lowered through a hatch in the fore end, and rotated to give thrust in the required direction. Although bow thrusters are used in some commercial craft, they are fixed in the sides and are driven by engines forward. The hydraulic drive permits this same type of system, without the added noise and vibration of engines forward, and with easy withdrawal of the propellers for normal motoring conditions.

For the very high-speed race boats or the large ocean-going fast motor yacht, jet propulsion using a gas jet mounted in the after end with air intakes down the yacht's side would have great advantage. The craft can be fitted with a small diesel and pod drive for manoeuvring in crowded waters and when motoring in the open sea the propeller pod can be withdrawn giving very little appendage drag as a fair closing plate is slid across the propeller opening. The jet engines are not dependent on the craft being in contact with the sea surface at all times, a great problem for the high-speed craft. These jet engines deliver high thrust for weight but should be sound insulated from the main accommodation area. This type of craft would be used solely as a high-speed commuting type, as both noise and wind when running at speed would not permit the passengers to wander about on deck. The hull can be fitted with small wings enabling some aerodynamic lift to be achieved, reducing the slamming loads as the craft hits the oncoming wave.

Powering and propulsion in the auxiliary sailing yacht requires special design attention. The IOR has led to many odd powering arrangements, such as

Fig. 6.4. Resistance chart for different propeller types.

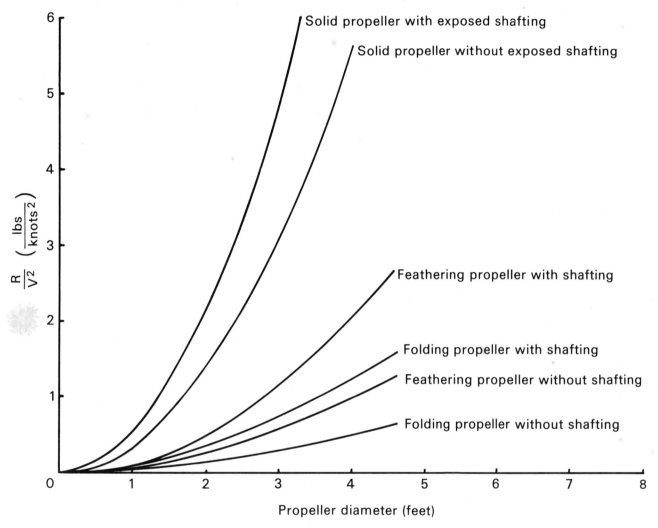

mounting the engines as far aft or forward as possible, as a rating allowance is given on the distance of the engine from the longitudinal centre of gravity of the yacht. Such odd engine arrangements are rarely beneficial to the design and have only been practicable since the advent of hydraulic drive. The two-bladed propeller is used fairly universally on the modern sailing racing yacht in order to reduce propeller drag to a minimum. The propeller may be of the folding type which gives least resistance, or is fixed vertically in line with the deadwood or in front of the skeg, offering slightly more resistance (Fig. 6.4). Folding types rely on centrifugal force to open the propeller on shaft rotation. The two-bladed propeller has the disadvantage that it rotates through a very uneven water pressure causing high-bearing friction and some degree of propeller-induced vibration. The three-bladed type reduces these problems but usually offers higher resistance under sail. Undoubtedly for the motor sailer the variable-pitch three-bladed propeller is the best compromise. This type may be set at a feathering angle when the engine is not in use to offer least resistance, and for low speeds and manoeuvring in crowded waters where maximum thrust is required quickly the pitch can be set at the optimum. It might also be possible to design a folding three- or four-bladed propeller, reducing the resistance but eliminating some of the problems of the two-bladed types.

Undoubtedly the future will reveal electric propulsion in auxiliary yachts, particularly motor sailers or cruising craft where displacement is not critical. Bulb keels in the larger yachts might be fitted with hydraulic or possibly electric motors, and in the case of the latter, with the batteries stowed along the centreline just above the ballast keel. These electric motors low down have the advantage that maximum thrust can be achieved from the propeller, which is sufficiently far from the surface to prevent cavitation. This system of engine housing was used in *Bras D'Or* at the base of the foils, with gas turbines being used to deliver the high power required. It is important to note that engine-room ventilation will become increasingly important with the advent of battery-driven machinery as the hydrogen admitted from lead/acid batteries becomes very dangerous if allowed to accumulate. Air intake and exhaust for diesel machinery can be a difficult problem for the cruising motor sailer as the engines are stowed away under cockpit soles so that as little accommodation space as possible is lost. Exhaust gases can be vented up the mast to take them well clear of the cockpit and accommodation.

Great attention should be given to engine access and ease of engine removal for the cruising motor yacht. Often, in recently designed craft, if engines have to be removed much of the superstructure has to be cut away to allow an easy crane hoist. If it is not possible to arrange engine removal hatches above the larger diesels, sufficient access should be provided to the sump to allow a bottom end overhaul to be carried out. Also clearance should be provided above the engine for piston withdrawal. Where it is necessary to have the engine as low as possible, so that sump removal becomes impossible without lifting, it might be possible in the case of metal or GRP construction to fit access hatches in the bottom of the boat.

Designers should give special attention to engine girder strength. There has been a tendency over the years to decrease steadily the length of engine girders, and in the case of auxiliary yachts these girders often are not supported sufficiently transversely. This bad tendency has led to stress vibration cracks in shell plating and girder welds in the case of metal boats, and some delamination in GRP. Aft bearings may be soon worn out even though flexible couplings are fitted due to the lack of longitudinal rigidity in the larger yachts. Another feature requiring special note is the attachment of stern glands in the case of GRP yachts. Often the metal gland is passed through the hull and laminated over at the ends. Inevitably, with the vibration in this area, the bond between the metal and the GRP is broken down, particularly if the gland heats up excessively due to misalignment, all resulting in water seeping in by way of the gland joint. In designing the powering system of the modern motor yacht, the designer has many features to take into account including the choice of material and the type of powering and propulsion.

7
Materials and construction

Over the last twenty years the materials of yacht construction have undergone great change and the whole technology has leaned towards the use of GRP. The main reason for this is an economic one. Most would agree as far as the aesthetics of boat construction are concerned that the timber yacht has a far more pleasant 'feel' than its clinical GRP counterpart. But it is becoming increasingly more important to reduce the labour spent in construction, fitting out and repair and until recently boatbuilding has been a very labour-intensive industry. Consider for instance the great difference in time spent in producing a 40-ft yacht in wood by traditional methods and GRP. At one time an owner would order his vessel a year to a year and a half before handover date from an average yard employing six or seven men; the lofting, setting out, framing and planking of the hull took about eight months. Yet the hull and deck of a GRP yacht takes two weeks to mould and fit. However, to this time for the GRP vessel should be added a proportion of the time for making the plug and the mould. Although the construction of GRP yachts is essentially a less skilled task, the initial building of a fair plug from which the mould is taken is every bit as skilled as the craft of conventional boatbuilding and takes nearly as long. For the sake of argument, an average of twenty-five hulls may be taken from a 40-ft mould, giving an additional 1·3 weeks to be added to the hull moulding time as the proportion of the pattern construction time.

Steel construction might also be compared; however, steel boats of 40 ft length were relatively unusual twenty years ago. But steel and light alloy yachts are becoming more popular as welding technology advances. The chief problem in building the 40-ft sailing yacht in steel, and to a greater extent alloy, is the avoidance of welding distortion in the thin topside plating. There have been many steel yachts built recently to restricted scantlings and of light displacement for racing, but requiring half a ton of fillers to make the topsides fair!

The construction time for a metal boat hull averages about four months. Thus it is more competitive than traditional wood boatbuilding but less than GRP construction if more than three boats have to be built to the same design. Therefore, metal construction, particularly light alloy, should be borne in mind more often when considering the one-off racing yacht. There are already signs that designers are realising the merit of this material as more light alloy racers are being built, and the advantages of this construction are discussed more fully under the relevant heading below. Table 7.1 summarises the properties of these various materials. It is wrong merely to compare specific strengths, i.e. tensile strength over specific gravity, as is done by many designers in selecting materials. One of the most important properties of the material required for boat construction is an ability to resist deflection. The method of carrying out this calculation is shown below.

Thickness is the most important feature for the resistance of deflection. If deflection exceeds $t/2$ the material is subjected to membrane stress; in other words the plate is acting like a drum skin, a large proportion of the stress due to the normal force being transmitted through the plate as tensions in its own plane. Our 40-ft steel sailing yacht would have topsides of about $\frac{3}{16}$ in with frame spacing at about 16 in; thus to subject this material to membrane stress the deflection between frames would have to be about 0·1 in or span/160. We do not usually consider such things as membrane stresses for timber construction, as the hull planking for the wood boat would be about 1 in thick, and it is very unusual to exceed this deflection limit and would be disastrous if the deflections reached $\frac{1}{2}$ in between

Table 7.1. A comparison of the physical and mechanical properties of the materials commonly used in boatbuilding

Material	Specific gravity	Ultimate tensile strength $\times 10^3$ (lb/in^2)	Specific strength $\times 10^3$ (lb/in^2)	Ultimate compressive strength $\times 10^3$ (lb/in^2)	Ultimate shear strength $\times 10^3$ (lb/in^2)	Young's modulus $\times 10^6$ (lb/in^2)	Thickness for equal deflection (in)
African mahogany	0·46	7	15·2	6·7	2·0 parallel to grain	1·1	0·97
GRP (chopped strand mat)	1·40	13	9·3	20	10·5	1·0	1·00
GRP (woven rovings)	1·60	32	20·0	14	14·0 across fibres	1·9	0·81
Aluminium alloy (ASTM 5083 or BS N8)	2·70	46	17·0	44	27·0	10·3	0·46
Mild steel	7·80	70	9·0	68	35·0	29·0	0·33
Ferrocement (high mesh content)	2·60	0·9	0·3	7	0·12	0·5	1·30

frames in a conventional planked hull. Again the same criterion for membrane stress applies to ferrocement yachts as to wood.

Most people following the development and construction of yachts realise the interest now being shown in ferrocement construction. This is by no means a new material, as the first ferrocement yacht was built in the Mediterranean in the 1920s. New Zealand and the USA have taken the lead in this form of construction. This is a very labour-intensive form of building during the plastering-up stage, and the authors have known of some sixty plasterers working on one 70-ft fishing boat, leading to extreme overcrowding! However, this stage only lasts for a few days. Probably the main reason for the surge in popularity is the apparent ease of construction for the do-it-yourself enthusiasts. But it is still a skilled job to set a fair steel framework and mesh, and perhaps even more skilled to plaster correctly so that

the material is forced well into the mesh to eliminate the air gaps which often exist in this form of construction, leading to crazing and unsightly rust seepage. Much development is being concentrated on new cements, including those reinforced with glass or hemp. One of the difficulties of a homogeneous, isotropic material of this nature is that stress cracks tend to run for long distances once started, and the small fibres of glass or hemp have the property of acting as crack-arresters in the cement.

GRP Construction

Throughout the discussions and comparisons of the various types of materials, a 40-ft sailing yacht is used as the example. The usual method of construction in GRP is by the badly nicknamed 'bucket and brush' method. A team of laminators is

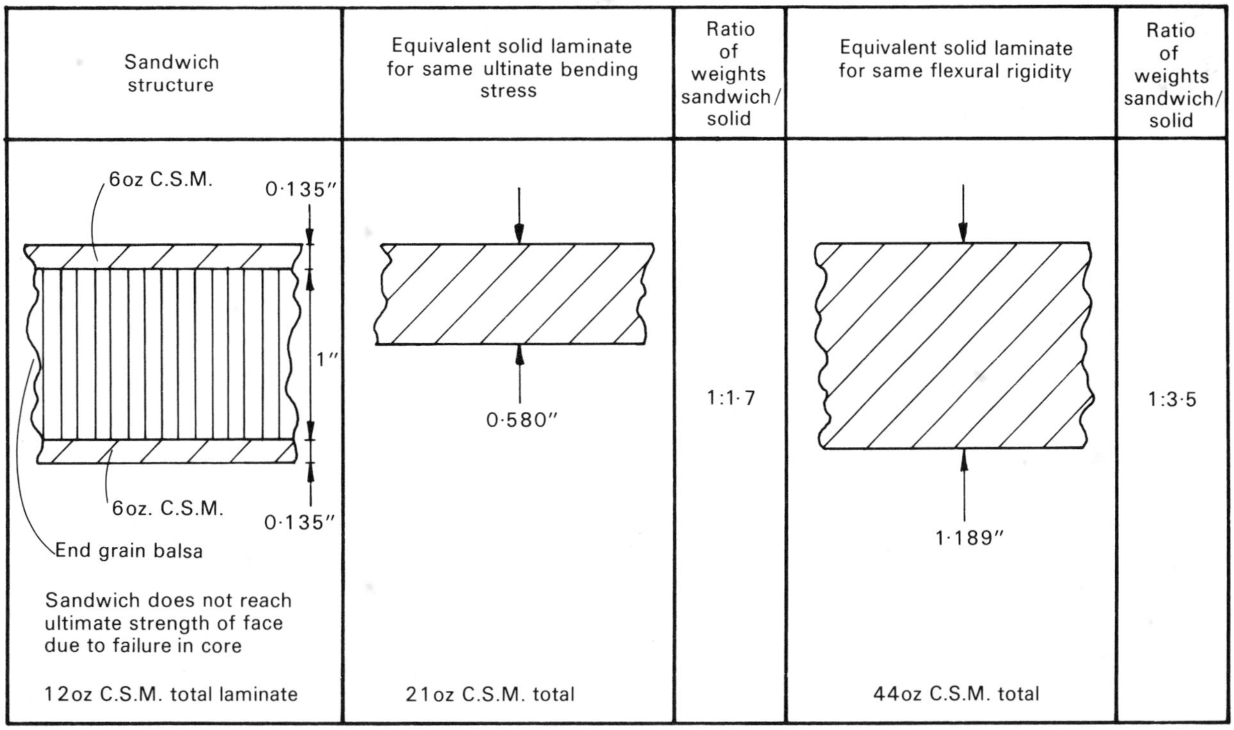

Fig. 7.1. Comparison of solid GRP laminate to a GRP
sandwich structure using 6 lb/ft³ density end grain balsa
core material. Care should be taken in the design of the
sandwich structure to ensure that sufficient compressive
and shear strengths exist throughout the different materials.

Sandwich structure	Equivalent solid laminate for same ultinate bending stress	Ratio of weights sandwich/ solid	Equivalent solid laminate for same flexural rigidity	Ratio of weights sandwich/ solid
6oz C.S.M. 0·135" 1" 6oz. C.S.M. 0·135" End grain balsa Sandwich does not reach ultimate strength of face due to failure in core 12oz C.S.M. total laminate	0·580" 21oz C.S.M. total	1:1·7	1·189" 44oz C.S.M. total	1:3·5

given pieces of glass fibre material, either chopped
strand mat consisting of random fibres of glass about
4 in long held together by a binder, or woven roving
which looks like a coarse cloth and is held together
by the weave. Weights of CSM material are
expressed in oz per sq ft or grams per sq m. Weights
are used in selecting the type of material as the
strength of the laminate is proportional to the
amount of glass. CSM is often used in conjunction
with woven rovings (WR). To make things even more
confusing, weights of woven roving are expressed in
oz per sq yd or grams per sq m. Thus when
comparing basic weights of glass, but not strengths
of laminates, the weights of the WR should be·
divided by nine to convert to imperial units.

The designer calculates the various combinations
of layers and types of reinforcement and stiffening to
suit the hull and its intended structure.

The laminating team is given these glass materials
and a bucket of resin with catalyst added. They then
proceed to apply material in the order specified,
taking care when rolling out the resin and glass to
eliminate air bubbles. This is often an unpleasant
job, particularly in confined spaces such as inside
tanks, as the gaseous styrene emitted can cause facial
burns and sore eyes. It is very important under such
circumstances to have a good supply of fresh warm
air piped into the confined space. It will be realised
that this form of construction is labour-intensive,
and the following ideas and methods of construction
should be considered by builders to help reduce
labour costs. Undoubtedly, many of these ideas will

be used in the future and some of them are being tried successfully today.

Sandwich Construction

As shown earlier, resistance to deflection is proportional to thickness cubed and modulus of elasticity. GRP chopped strand mat construction having a modulus of about 1 million pounds per square inch (p.s.i.) has only $\frac{1}{29}$ the resistance to deflection of mild steel. However, the 40-ft yacht would have a bottom hull about $\frac{3}{8}$ in thick in GRP compared to $\frac{3}{16}$ in in steel. Thus the t^3 factor gives a ratio of resistance to deflection of 8 : 1 steel to GRP, resulting in a GRP yacht deflecting approximately $3\frac{1}{2}$ times as much as its steel sister ship for the same frame spacing. It has been the practice for many yards to eliminate the use of frames to support the hull as this is a costly part of the construction. If the time taken for laminating shell, frames and intersections such as tank corners is compared with a properly framed 70-ft motor yacht, the time taken would be of the order 1 : 5 : 8 respectively. But the elimination of framing has had disastrous effects. Many offshore racing boats of 35 ft upwards are suffering damage due to excessive deflection in the forward area, particularly if this pounding area has little curvature. It is not enough to rely solely on joinery to support the shell in these high stress areas. Many owners complain that their doors and lockers do not shut properly: this is not often due to swelling of unseasoned timber, but to movement and distortion of the hull itself. The problem is how to construct a rigid GRP shell economically, and sandwich construction is one of the obvious solutions to this.

A sandwich structure in the case of GRP consists of two skins of the laminate separated by a low-density core material such as balsa, PVC foam or polyurethane foam. This sandwich structure offers almost the same resistance to deflection as its solid laminate counterpart, but with much less weight, as the core material has far lower density than the solid laminate (Fig. 7.1). The main problem is to obtain an efficient bond between the hull exterior laminate and the sandwich core when using a mould. It can be seen from Fig. 7.2 that having laid up the exterior laminate, which for our 40-ft yacht would be about the equivalent of 8 oz of CSM, the sandwich core is then bedded on to the last layer of wet mat, the degree of bedding being dependent on the pressure applied to the core. This pressure may be affected by use of weights or a pressure bag acting like a large balloon forced against the core. It is difficult to achieve more than a 60 per cent effective bond between the core and outer skin due to air being trapped between the two outer faces. The bond between the core and the inner skin is usually far better as the laminate is applied to the core, so the initial layers are carefully rolled out eliminating any air entrapped.

One-off GRP sandwich yachts are being built using a foam core set on moulds and laminating both the exterior and interior skins on to the foam form. This method saves the cost of a mould, which for say a 75-ft sailing vessel may be as much as three times the cost of the hull and deck. Undoubtedly this method of building will increase in the future particularly as it is suitable for do-it-yourself enthusiasts. The main disadvantage with this construction is that it is virtually impossible to obtain as fair a surface as that achieved using a female mould. It requires many hours of sanding and filling of the last layer of GRP laminate to obtain a good finish. The following ideas are suggested solutions to these problems.

Firstly, the conventional sandwich structure using a female mould should be disregarded in its present

Fig. 7.2. Typical sandwich lay-up system.

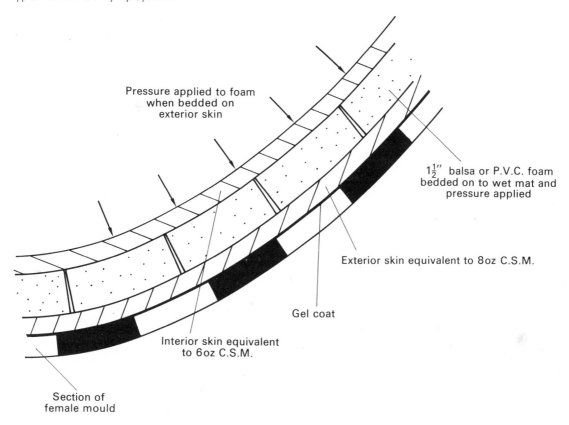

Pressure applied to foam
when bedded on
exterior skin

$1\frac{1}{2}''$ balsa or P.V.C. foam
bedded on to wet mat and
pressure applied

Exterior skin equivalent to 8oz C.S.M.

Gel coat

Interior skin equivalent
to 6oz C.S.M.

Section of
female mould

approach to design. In order to effect a good bond between outer skin and core the answer lies in applying the foam core as a liquid, thus ensuring that no air is trapped between the outer skin and core. When the chemists develop a high-density predictable foaming plastic such as PVC, this will be applied to the inside of the outer skin using a brush or mechanical dispenser; this core would then be left to foam to nearly constant thickness and then the inner skin would be laminated over. To avoid excessive delamination between skin and foam in the case of impact damage, small webs may be tied between the inner and outer skins by foaming up in panels and laminating the inner skin over on to the outer before continuing the next panel (Fig. 7.3).

In the future it should become possible to purchase large sheets of GRP laminate to the required thickness much as one buys sheets of plywood; these may be either single skin or sandwiches with various degrees of curvature. Using such panels, boats will be constructed in a way similar to present-day steel fabrication but instead of welding, these plastic panels will be glued, probably using a mechanical dispenser feeding on a strip of wet laminate at the joint. It will be possible to supply these panels laminated to a very high quality, i.e. with a high glass/resin ratio, with gel coat applied to one side, and the edges scarphed back and a strip applied in the bonding area which may be peeled away to reveal a slightly uncured resin

Fig. 7.3. A sandwich structure incorporating shear webs between inner and outer skins by laminating in sections.

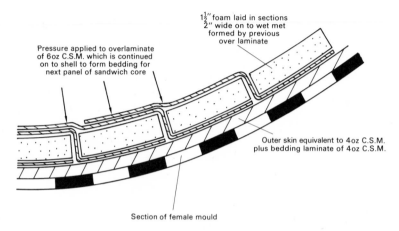

1½" foam laid in sections 2" wide on to wet met formed by previous over laminate

Pressure applied to overlaminate of 6oz C.S.M. which is continued on to shell to form bedding for next panel of sandwich core

Outer skin equivalent to 4oz C.S.M. plus bedding laminate of 4oz C.S.M.

Section of female mould

surface thus ensuring perfect bonding in way of the joints. This method is applicable particularly to shipbuilding (where a large percentage of the plates used need have no curvature) and also to yachts of the hard chine form.

Another method which will increase in popularity is the use of semi-stiff glass rods laid over sectional moulds in a similar way to the one-off sandwich foam construction.

It was mentioned above that the ratio of laminating times of shell to frames to intersections is approximately 1 : 5 : 8 for a 70-ft yacht; it will be thus realised that an extensively framed GRP yacht suitable for high speed purposes, though structurally sound, is extremely expensive to produce, and it will be necessary for the industry to find an alternative to this method. The best solution is undoubtedly the sandwich structure but it might be necessary to wait for several years before the chemists are able to produce a foam of the required properties.

A solution which is more applicable now is to laminate an internal skin incorporating frames, bulkhead landings, bunks and internal arrangements, and to bed this structure on to wet laminate. To ensure a good bond between these GRP skins an air extraction pump would be applied to the frames until sufficient air pressure, e.g. 2 p.s.i., is acting on the internal skin. All this internal structure would of course be laminated separately from the main structure in a female mould and would be made in sections of sizes most easily handled. For our 40-ft yacht it should be possible to fit this moulding in one piece using a slow-curing resin in the bedding laminate. This is an extension of the system used by some yards to rely on the internal moulding for stiffening.

In using material such as GRP, operations may be carried out and shapes produced which are not possible in welded steel or aluminium. Thus the ship designer when posed with the problem of designing a GRP craft should completely reappraise his approach to the task. It is not enough simply to design a ship of, say, 160 ft by taking a shell and attaching framing and to expect such a structure to hold together under severe buckling stresses. The peeling stress of the joint between the frames and the skin will be the limiting factor, as only relatively low stresses can be supported by this joint, the material of the shell and the frames will never be subjected to their load-carrying capacities. This is a

Fig. 7.4. Section of 160-ft motor yacht with integral frames. Section through bottom panel showing stiffening members incorporated into hull moulding.

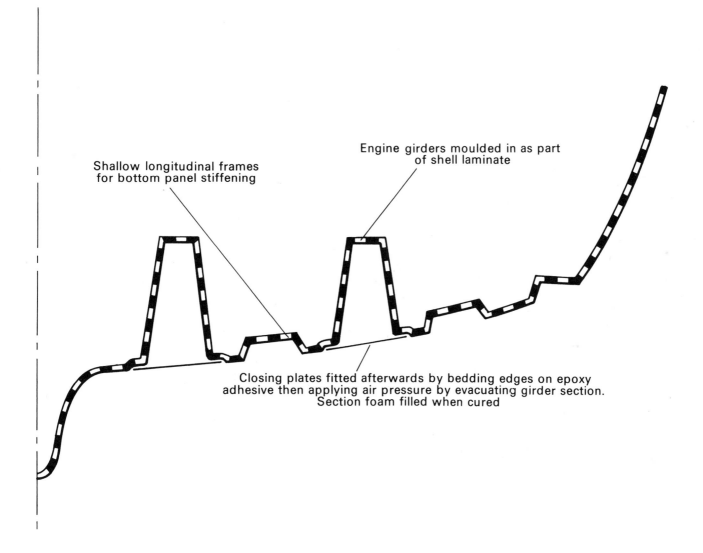

Shallow longitudinal frames for bottom panel stiffening

Engine girders moulded in as part of shell laminate

Closing plates fitted afterwards by bedding edges on epoxy adhesive then applying air pressure by evacuating girder section. Section foam filled when cured

design problem for all types of boats and ships of increasing length due to the hogging, buckling loads in the bottom structure. A solution lies in moulding in the framework as part of the hull shell itself, and fitting closing plates over these hull recesses in way of frames and girders where a smooth external skin is required; this ensures continuity between the shell skin and the frame webs. It would be completely impractical to consider this method of construction in steel shipbuilding, but GRP construction lends itself ideally to this method.

Another cheap and relatively simple solution to

solving the shell deflection problem is the moulding-in of longitudinal corrugations throughout the length of the yacht (Fig. 7.4). This was virtually impossible before the advent of GRP as it is particularly difficult to weld a metal hull with such a series of small panels, or to build in wood without leaks occurring at the joints. These corrugations have additional advantages in slow-speed workboats as they help to reduce roll when not underway. If the corners of the corrugations are built up sufficiently there is no worry about wear and tear of these points.

Undoubtedly the future holds some exciting developments in fibre-reinforced plastics. Carbon fibre has been introduced recently in limited quantities into GRP laminates to increase strength and rigidity. At present the cost of boron and carbon fibres restricts use to limited applications. The properties of carbon fibre laminates are shown in Table 7.2. It can be seen from the chart that the great advantage of incorporating carbon fibre in glass panels is that it helps to reduce deflection, which is a major problem as this material has a low modulus. There is little point at present in introducing these fibres into, say, longitudinals and frame faces, as unidirectional glass material having very high strength and modulus properties in one direction may be used to great advantage along these areas, because virtually all of the tensile stress runs in the direction of the girder. A comparison between the tensile strength and modulus of unidirectional glass and CSM laminates is also given in Table 7.3.

It can be seen that unidirectional GRP has about four times the tensile strength of a CSM laminate and three times the modulus in the direction of the glass orientation. But there is virtually no strength perpendicular to the glass filaments and this material should be used only where the direction of stress is accurately known. Unidirectional material may be used in conjunction with more isotropic materials like CSM over the shell for limited applications such as spanning frames, when it is known that high stress runs between supporting members of minimum separation. Fig. 7.5 shows how a combination of unidirectional glass and multidirectional material may be used on the bottom of high-speed planing boats to achieve a minimum weight structure. The unidirectional glass could be replaced by carbon fibre to give an even greater reduction in weight.

Thus it may be seen that there exists a very promising future for the development of reinforced plastics in both yacht and ship construction. In addition to reinforced plastics the development of isotropic plastics, such as are used in everyday articles, will increase steadily, enabling injection moulding techniques to be adopted for small boats up to 20 ft in length. The restriction in size of craft capable of being produced by this technique is governed by the high cost of producing the steel moulds required for this process, but undoubtedly more runabouts such as dinghies and tenders will be moulded in isotropic plastics.

Steel and Light Alloy Construction

Small boat construction in steel and light alloys has not been realised to its full potential. Only recently, with the advent of improved argon arc welding, have light alloy boats been produced in any number. It is not feasible yet to design a steel yacht of competitive performance to, say, wood, under about 50 ft in length, due to weight considerations. The limiting factor for the minimum acceptable plating thickness for shell plating is $\frac{3}{16}$ in because below this, welding distortions become difficult to control and little margin is left for corrosion (though with modern coatings this is less important). As the relative

Table 7.2 Properties of carbon fibre laminates

Laminate type	Specific gravity	Tensile strength $\times 10^3$ (lb/in^2)	Young's modulus $\times 10^6$ (lb/in^2)
GRP (chopped strand mat)	1·4	13	1·0
GRP (unidirectional glass)	1·9	60	3·0
Pure carbon fibre in epoxy resin	1·8	300	40
Isotropic GRP laminate with 10% carbon fibres	1·5	70	6·0

The most useful property of a limited application of carbon fibres is the increasing of Young's modulus, thus providing greater panel stiffness.

Table 7.3 Typical physical and mechanical properties of reinforced polyester plastic using different types of glass reinforcement

Type of reinforcement	Glass content % weight	Specific gravity	Tensile strength $\times 10^3$ (lb/in^2)	Compressive strength $\times 10^3$ (lb/in^2)	Flexural strength $\times 10^3$ (lb/in^2)	Flexural modulus $\times 10^6$ (lb/in^2)	Impact strength Izod, un-notched
Chopped strand mat (CSM)	30	1·4	13	20	18	1·0	14
Woven rovings (WR)	38	1·6	32	14	30	2·0	21
Cloth	50	1·7	40	30	50	2·1	23
Unidirectional rovings (UD)	65	1·9	60	40	70	3·5	35

densities of light alloy to steel are approximately 0·4 to 1, it is more feasible to plate an upper hull in a reasonable plating thickness in this material. The bottom plating for a 40-ft racing boat would be of the order of $\frac{1}{4}$ in. Higher tensile steels are available, making steel construction as competitive as any of the other materials, but these are very expensive. The nickel/steel alloys with over 15 per cent nickel can have ultimate tensile strengths of 250,000 p.s.i., compared with normal steel used for ship and boat construction which has a tensile strength of 65,000 p.s.i. These high-nickel steels are well suited to welding but are vulnerable to stress corrosion cracking and hydrogen embrittlement, requiring very careful coating with plastic paints to prevent failure. However, if expense is no object, construction in this material is very well suited for craft such as racing power boats. The hydrofoil

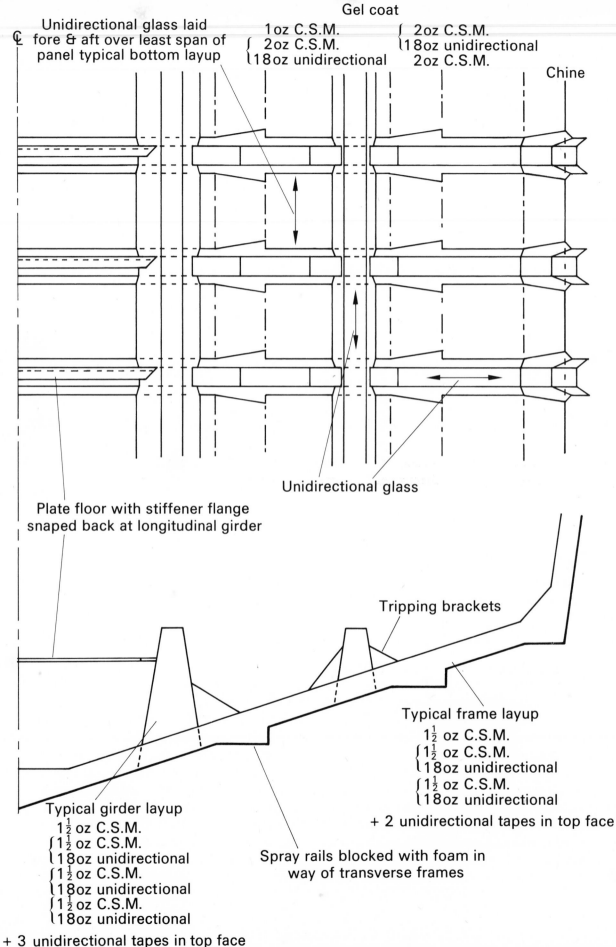

Gel coat

Unidirectional glass laid
fore & aft over least span of
panel typical bottom layup

{ 1oz C.S.M.
  2oz C.S.M.
  18oz unidirectional

{ 2oz C.S.M.
  18oz unidirectional
  2oz C.S.M.

Chine

Unidirectional glass

Plate floor with stiffener flange
snaped back at longitudinal girder

Tripping brackets

Typical frame layup
1½ oz C.S.M.
{ 1½ oz C.S.M.
  18oz unidirectional
{ 1½ oz C.S.M.
  18oz unidirectional

+ 2 unidirectional tapes in top face

Spray rails blocked with foam in
way of transverse frames

Typical girder layup
1½ oz C.S.M.
{ 1½ oz C.S.M.
  18oz unidirectional
{ 1½ oz C.S.M.
  18oz unidirectional
{ 1½ oz C.S.M.
  18oz unidirectional

+ 3 unidirectional tapes in top face

Fig. 7.5. Lay-up of high-speed motor yacht. Typical structure for 40-ft high-speed GRP hull indicating the use of glass orientation to give minimum weight for strength. Carbon fibres could be incorporated into the shell lay-up to give greater stiffness or more weight-saving.

HMCS *Bras D'Or* (see page 56), had foils manufactured of such a steel to withstand the very high-pressure loading without excessive weight restriction. Using this steel, she was able to maintain a speed of 60 knots in three to four feet waves – a truly remarkable performance.

One of the first queries raised with the designer when a boat is to be built of alloy, and to a lesser extent steel, is the corrosion problem and in particular electrolytic action. The corrosion resistance of alloys suitable for marine use has improved greatly over the years. It may not be realised that the first use of aluminium for boatbuilding dates back to the nineteenth century. The first seagoing hull of any note was a 40-ft steam yacht, the *Mignon*, built in France in 1891. The French navy in 1894 built a 60-ft aluminium steam yacht capable of over 21 knots and driven by a 300-h.p. engine. Since then high-strength magnesium alloys have been developed which are particularly applicable to marine use. The first boat of any size to be built of the new magnesium alloy was the 55-ft cruiser *Diana II*, built in 1931 in England. The hull was plated mainly with 10-gauge material 0·134 in (3·5 mm). Perhaps a little thin by today's standards, *Diana II* is still in service after all these years. Aluminium alloy construction developed a bad name when many firms built in cheaper alloys having sufficient strength but containing small quantities of copper, fatal for marine use. Often these alloys came from scrapped aircraft after the war. Marine alloys are superb boatbuilding materials, particularly where a high strength/weight ratio is required proving to be more cost effective than timber. However, plating a boat out in thin alloy sheets requires a great deal of skill and there are still only a handful of yards around the world capable of producing a fair boat. Now that the 12-Metres for the America's Cup may be built in alloy, many owners of smaller racing yachts are tending to favour this material and more builders are getting practice in plating-up by building ocean racers.

An alloy yacht may be left completely unpainted quite satisfactorily, and it is of interest to note that the unpainted hull will usually experience less deep pitting due to corrosion than the painted hull. This may be explained by the fact that, in the case of the unpainted hull, the whole area is subjected to the 'electrolytic potential' as opposed to the concentrated corrosion over a small area where the paint surface has been scratched away. The surface of the alloy holds a very thin coating of aluminium oxide which is an extremely inert material, and if this oxide is scratched away it immediately reforms. Occasionally a catastrophic corrosion of an alloy hull occurs, causing fright among the yachting fraternity owning boats of this material. This is almost without exception due to galvanic action and is caused usually by the presence of copper and/or an electrical leak, resulting in severe wasting of the alloy of the higher negative or less noble potential. The owners of aluminium yachts should always take care to use the correct antifouling – that is, one that does not contain copper products. The most suitable antifoulings for aluminium usually contain tin having no detrimental effect on the hull. Also, care should be taken in mooring alongside steel jetties and steel craft with copper antifoul, or worse still, timber boats with copper sheathing.

And what developments may be expected? The corrosion resistance and strength properties of the alloys will steadily increase. At present, the best alloy for marine purposes is alloy N.8 British Standard, equivalent to 5083 American Society for Testing and Materials (ASTM) having an ultimate tensile strength of 46,000 p.s.i. It is better than steel in weight for strength. However, these alloys have a modulus of approximately 10×10^6 p.s.i. compared with steel of three times that value, so great care has to be taken to consider deflection and buckling stability when designing in this material. As a rule, materials of low moduli require closer frame spacing than normal.

Welding techniques have improved greatly over the last decade and will continue to do so, enabling fast and efficient welding without heat distortion. When welding alloy it is important to prevent the protective oxide from forming, otherwise the joint will not be structurally effective. Today this is carried out by shielding the metal in the inert gas argon. Also, to avoid heat distortion in very thin plating, a factor becoming increasingly important as the strength of the alloys increases, thus leading to thinner plating, the temperature required for welding should be reached very quickly in the localised area and the remaining plate should be shielded from this high temperature. Automatic welding machines providing shielding and heat sinks will be developed, possibly permitting alloys as thin as $\frac{1}{16}$ in (1·5 mm) to be welded without distortion. It is unlikely that these alloys will be required for bottom plating, but they could be most useful for superstructure design where top weight should be saved if at all possible.

As mentioned earlier, very high tensile steels are available but generally suffer problems such as severe stress corrosion. Recently, a steel known as Corten has been used in marine construction, with yacht designers and builders claiming great advantages. However, Corten is a steel having high-corrosion resistance in atmospheric conditions but not in a marine environment. It was developed for exposed use in buildings and can be observed in high-rise buildings. Paint adheres better to this steel, but this is the only real advantage that can be claimed for its use in boat construction.

Stainless steel technology is developing rapidly and one may expect that within the next decade the cost of stainless steels will become more competitive, enabling all-stainless boats to be built. It is worth mentioning that there is stainless and 'stainless'! Stainless steels vary considerably in corrosion resistance, and the higher tensile stainless steels tend to have worse resistance; these usually suffer crevice corrosion. This material, like aluminium alloy, relies upon a protective coat of oxide. If the steel is subjected to an oxygen-free environment corrosion may be rapid. Crevice corrosion occurs in recesses where oxygen has been used up and fresh oxygen cannot reach the surface of the material. The reader may observe this by looking at stainless steel fittings or fastenings, and seeing that rust streaks only spring from obscure crevices.

Wood Construction

It is often not realised that timber construction has undergone a steady revolution. This has been brought about by the development of new adhesives. The days of steaming timbers to bend them to a required shape have gone, as it is now possible to laminate timber to achieve the same effect with greater guarantee of strength. A modern laminated timber has far greater strength than a solid piece of the same dimensions. In a solid piece shakes or cracks may run for considerable length but in the case of the laminated structure these, if at all present, are restrained in length, and the timber is not pre-stressed into a curve.

Among the most recent developments in glue technology has been the introduction of epoxy resins. These were first developed by Castar in Switzerland and Greenlee in the United States in the 1930s. They are similar to phenolic and polyester resins (GRP contains polyester resin) in that they are all thermo-setting materials. A catalyst is added to the resin to increase the speed of chemical reaction forming the plastic or hard glue. Epoxy resins, apart from their adhesive strength, have the following advantageous properties: low shrinkage, easy handling, fast curing, water and chemical resistance, and versatility. The epoxy resin differs from many other resin glues in that no byproducts are evolved during curing, and cure-shrinkage is of the order of 0·0001 in per in length, or $\frac{1}{10}$ of a thou'.

The earlier urea formaldehyde glues commonly used before the development of these latest products became nearly obsolete when the resorcinols were developed. These adhesives conform to the British and American Standard weather- and boil-proof test (WBP) and the gap-filling requirement. Before these plastic glues, adhesives were made from bone glues, soya beans, vegetable starch, cellulose and blood albumen. It is important that a glue should be chosen for the particular application. Phenolic adhesives are suited to timber of low moisture content. Thus they are ideally suited to plywood production. They are best applied hot and under pressure as is the case in plywood manufacture, but this is not always possible in boatbuilding. The urea formaldehyde glues mentioned earlier have the main advantage of considerable time-saving. They are usually supplied as fine white powder soluble in water, in concentrations of between 50 and 20 per cent forming a syrup. The hardener and catalyst are supplied in two types: one where the glue is put on one surface and the hardener on the other, the action starting when the joint is closed, the other having the glue and catalyst mixed before application. Urea formaldehyde resin glues should not be used where there are alkalis or acids present: be careful with washing powder and paint strippers! This glue, unlike the resorcinols or epoxies, is moisture resistant but not weather and boil-proof.

The epoxy glues first discussed are not only able to fasten timber very strongly but will also glue alloy, brass, Perspex and difficult timbers such as teak and other slightly oily hardwoods. The best bond with these hardwoods is made by removing the surface oil through washing with carbon tetrachloride and allowing to dry before gluing. When using epoxies the pressure need be adequate only to ensure close contact of the fitting surfaces, and the glues are thus extremely efficient for cold-moulded construction. However, the cost of these epoxy glues is greater than that of the phenolics and considerably more than the urea formaldehyde and bone glues.

Cold and hot moulded construction with the right timbers is still the highest strength-for-weight construction material used in boatbuilding with alloy running a fairly close second. It is a pity that this form of construction, due to its labour-intensive nature, is not more widely practised. However, it is undoubtedly one of the finest forms for the one-off racing yacht and many superb examples such as *Crusade* and *Outlaw*, have been built using the cold-moulding technique. Many of the world's fastest power boats are constructed like this, and the use of very light timbers such as poplar (though lacking the durability of the more conventional timbers) is recommended.

As was mentioned in the GRP section, sandwich construction forms the highest rigidity for least weight of any type of construction. It is therefore suggested that a cold-moulded hull built in a female mould using a balsa core between light skins of African mahogany glued with an epoxy would produce a very light but strong structure. Fig. 7.6 gives the order of rigidity and strength that would be expected from such a construction, and the equivalent thickness of other materials. The major disadvantages of this type of structure are that repair

Fig. 7.6. Properties of wood sandwich structure. It can be
seen that a useful weight-saving over solid timber can be
achieved.

Wood sandwich structure	Equivalent thickness for equal ultimate stress	Ratio of weight sandwich / solid	Equivalent thickness for equal flexural rigidity	Ratio of weight sandwich / solid
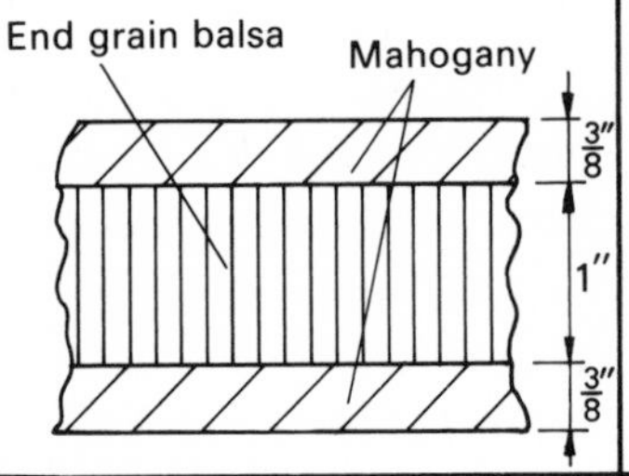 End grain balsa — Mahogany — 3/8" 1" 3/8"	Mahogany 1·47"	1:1·5	Mahogany 1·65"	1:1·6
	G.R.P. (C.S.M.) 1·08"	1:3·4	G.R.P. (C.S.M.) 1·81"	1:5·7
	Aluminium alloy 0·56"	1:3·5	Aluminium alloy 0·84"	1:5·2
	Mild steel 0·47"	1:8·4	Mild steel 0·59"	1:10·5

is somewhat awkward and difficult, and impact resistance of the outer skin is less than that of the solid material. However, weight saving of the order of 30 per cent could be expected in a Class I power boat hull.

Ferrocement Construction

Reinforced concrete construction achieved major popularity during the First World War, to enable cheap, small ships to be built quickly. Between 1917 and 1972 approximately 140,000 tons of these concrete ships were built. Unfortunately for this side of the industry, many poor examples were fabricated as the technology of reinforced concrete was very much in its infancy. The main problem at that time was the lack of suitable cement, causing crazing and rust. The ships were built very lightly and, although failures with this material were rarely so catastrophic, often the craft leaked after a year's service. There are, however, many examples from this period still afloat being used as houseboats and docks. By the early 1930s the technology of cement and concrete enabled the corrosion problem to be restricted, but the craft tended to be overweight, the skin on a 50-ft vessel being in the order of 2 in thick. In the early 1940s Professor Nervi and the firm Nervi & Bartoli developed a form of construction using a fine wire mesh fastened to main steel frames, the mesh being impregnated with cement mortar. Nervi first described the properties of the new material: 'The material created did not behave like normal concrete but presented all the mechanical characteristics of a homogeneous material; it could withstand great strains with formation of cracks in the cement mortar as a result of the subdivision of reinforcement.' In 1946 Nervi and Bartoli built a 165-ton motor sailer *Irene*. The boat proved the professor's ideas as she has stood up to test very well. The hull is 1·4 in thick and consists of three layers, two longitudinal and one transverse, of $\frac{1}{4}$-in steel bars at 4-in spacing and eight layers of mesh each weighing 0·24 lb per sq ft. The mortar was applied by hand from the inside of the hull and was forced through the mesh and smoothed out from the outside. Nervi stated, 'The hull was 5 per cent less than the weight of a similar wooden hull at a cost 40 per cent less.' It can be seen from Table 7.1 that ferrocement construction is not as good as most of the other materials in strength for weight, but due to the thickness of the shell the rigidity is high. In 1948 Nervi built a 38-ft ketch with a skin less than $\frac{1}{2}$-in thick, making her very competitive on all counts. After five years of extensive cruising her hull was still faultless.

The main disadvantage of ferrocement is that it is difficult to obtain a fair surface; however the cost is low and construction time quick compared with other materials. It is important that vessels should be built to a proper constructional design, for this material will soon craze and break up if insufficient thought is given to the panel rigidity and longitudinal bending strength. It is also important to take special care on the finishing of the hull; the surface is etch-primed first and then resin-based paints are used to ensure a good barrier to water penetration.

The popularity of ferrocement will continue to increase and the development of glass-reinforced and resin bonded cement mortars will enable the construction of even more competitive yachts.

In order to ease the labour intensity at the plastering stage, the use of cement spray guns forcing the material into the mesh with the plasterer following behind, consolidating and smoothing, will become increasingly popular. The material will never achieve the specific strengths and rigidities of the high-tensile alloys or the expensive carbon reinforced plastics, but will beat all other materials in cost. Within the next ten years hulls using this material will probably be constructed of approximately the same thickness as a GRP CSM hull, i.e. $\frac{3}{8}$-in thick bottom and slightly less thick topsides. As stainless steel becomes more competitive it is probable that a stainless steel framework with stainless wire mesh and glass and resin bonded mortars will enable a sophisticated and trustworthy boat to be produced. Without resorting to the cost of a mould, the hull finish will always remain inferior to that of say a mould-produced GRP hull. However, as discussed in the section on GRP sandwich construction, chine hulls could be constructed using thin panels of this material, bonded together with epoxy resin cement.

8
Accommodation, styling and equipment

There has been a steady change in outlook on internal arrangements. Until the late 1950s the procedure of approach to design of say a 40-ft sailing or motor yacht tended to concentrate on a pleasing profile, with the required hull form. Bulkheads and frames would be fitted as considered structurally necessary, with the general arrangements fitted around the structure.

Today the approach for the cruising yacht is usually to work on the general arrangement and then fit as many berths in as short a length as possible, with standing headroom an absolute necessity throughout. This approach has led to some ugly if functional craft. As far as the builders are concerned that is of little consequence, for a large percentage of those buying boats, especially those under 25-ft length, do not worry too much about aesthetic appeal. Although most would agree that long ends, a low coachroof and plenty of sheer, combined with low freeboard just aft of amidships, are necessary characteristics for a classically beautiful sailing yacht, when it is realised that five berths and 6 ft 2 in headroom cannot be achieved, the aesthetics give way to accommodation.

There will always be sailors with 'an eye for a boat', willing to sacrifice some accommodation for the proud knowledge that one has a beautiful little yacht, and that she is greatly admired in every port entered. But the mass-production 25-ft family cruiser, though clever in internal arrangement, can hardly be said to catch the eye as a handsome craft.

There is likely to be a strong reversion to the more pleasing profile while maintaining the present high standard of internal arrangements, though it is probable, with the depth of hulls decreasing as yachts become faster, that headroom will be reduced. This reaction could well be very strong, with a demand increasing for traditional local fishing types and similar characterful craft.

The Americans, and to some extent the Italians, have led the field in styling internal arrangements of GRP craft during the past ten years. However, the approach adopted by most British fitting-out yards is now very similar. This has come about because the arrangements are usually cheaper to fit, the American approach being to reduce the need for hand work to a minimum. Also, although a large number of the world's top yacht designers, both sail and power, work from the US their designs are moulded under licence or royalty systems throughout the world, leading to international standardisation and uniformity in certain types of craft. The influence on design of the Italians has come about because of a national flair for styling which is evident in their design of so many other items like houses, furniture and cars.

GRP construction has led to a rapid development of styling. It is expensive to produce curves in timber, particularly in two planes, but with GRP and moulded plastics generally it is as easy to produce a curved panel as a flat one. A beneficial offshoot of this is that structures can be made far more sound. A sharp corner cut in a timber panel is a potential failure point due to the high stress concentration in way of the small radius at the corner. There is no reason why GRP hatch openings should not be designed with well radiused corners, or completely circular or oval: after all, the body is not rectangular in cross-section. The same applies to some extent to plywood bulkheads: it was desirable perhaps to have rectangular openings when the bulkheads were constructed of tongue-and-groove timber, but how often does one see cracks running from the square corners in ply bulkhead openings due to the high stress loading at these points. This did not occur with the tongue-and-groove timber as there was sufficient movement between planks to relieve the stress.

GRP has also led to more daylight inside the

yacht because of the development of translucent resins. The yacht of the future could have a translucent cabin or deckhouse top with a shutter running in tracks, possibly electrically driven, which could be drawn across the deckhead when more privacy is required in port in the evening, or when the sun is strong overhead. This would have the added advantage of additional sound and temperature insulation at night.

The translucent property of resins might also be used to derive additional light from below – a development which would startle some owners with feelings of insecurity, as it could be felt the bottom was very thin and not capable of standing up to the pounding of the sea.

Window areas have increased steadily in size, particularly in motor yachts. The 84-ft schooner shown in Chapter 4 on motor sailers demonstrates how styling can incorporate large windows which enhance the profile. These windows can be made as strong as the surrounding GRP structure, so are perfectly safe; particularly as a breakwater can be fitted to the foredeck (where a yacht is likely to be subjected to violent seas if the windows are near deck level) at the forward end of the deckhouse. However, the increase in size should still be treated with some caution if there is a series of closely spaced windows. The naval architect should ensure that the frames are sufficiently strong so that the deckhouse top can support a static load of 0·3 lb per sq in or 43 lb per sq ft. Also sufficient racking stability should be provided by bulkheads or web frames running on to the window frames; these could be part of the aluminium or plastic frames bonded to the GRP deckhouse top. It is fortunate that some of the motor yachts produced today are likely to spend nearly all their life in marinas and not at sea in all weathers, for the deckhouses and bridges would undoubtedly fail early in the yacht's life.

The introduction of the all-GRP structure including internal moulding, together with the higher r.p.m. diesel engines, has increased the necessity for careful planning of engine-room layout and sound insulation. In motor yacht design the availability of variable shafting angle gearboxes enables the engines to be mounted at the transom of the yacht using outdrives, or V-drive shafting for the larger yachts, thus keeping the noisy engines well away from the living areas. One of the standard approaches to sound insulation is to use a high-density material such as lead, which absorbs the energy of the various frequencies at the bulkheads. Unfortunately this is not usually practical for fast motor yachts where due to the continuous search for performance, and weight restrictions do not permit ideal sound attenuators such as lead to be adopted. It is interesting to note that the motor sailer may be built as a far more comfortable craft in this respect as hull structure and insulation weight are far less critical than in motor yachts.

Metal pipes tend to be forgotten when sound insulation is arranged but these tend to transmit sound well. Thus, where possible, plastic pipes should be adopted or both tanks and pipes should be insulated with mineral wool. The future development of fireproof plastic/asbestos pipes will tend to eliminate this problem. The location of engine and type of mount are critical in eliminating noise. In motor sailing or auxiliary yachts the engines should be bolted directly to the lead keel thus transmitting all the vibrational energy to a large energy sink. In the motor yacht, flexible engine mounts and couplings should be used, preventing some of the vibration transmitting through to the hull via the engine seatings.

Ideally the engine room in both motor and sailing yachts should be lined with mineral wool, and all bulkheads in way of machinery should be rigidly

Fig. 8.1. Section through an engine-room sound insulator.

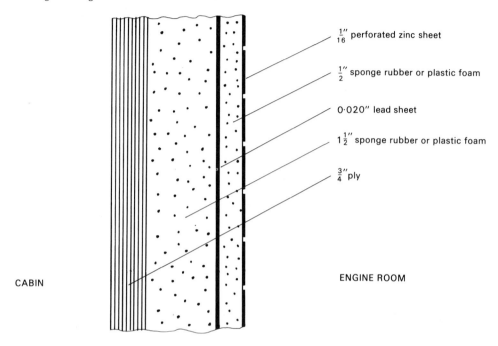

$\frac{1}{16}''$ perforated zinc sheet

$\frac{1}{2}''$ sponge rubber or plastic foam

0·020'' lead sheet

$1\frac{1}{2}''$ sponge rubber or plastic foam

$\frac{3}{4}''$ ply

CABIN

ENGINE ROOM

supported to prevent drumming. It is important for the designer to realise that structural stiffening in way of these bulkheads has to be more extensive than that required to support the hull. A typical section through an engine-room bulkhead is shown, giving reasonable sound installation (Fig. 8.1).

At night battery storage banks will help to reduce any noise as generators need then not be run. Unfortunately, where extensive air-conditioning is required at night AC generators have to be employed, increasing the necessity for careful design for sound insulation.

One very dangerous trend that has crept into yacht design, both sail and power, during the past fifteen years has been to ignore safe seagoing necessities such as structural considerations and seaworthiness, in order to exhibit the designers' talents in respect of furnishing arrangements and

unusual layout. It is all very well to have large open areas with cabins perhaps 13 ft long, but if sufficient strength and racking stability is to be maintained without excessive shell thickness, then bulkheads or web frames should be introduced at regular spacing. As a rule it is desirable to introduce these frames at 6-ft 6-in spacings, i.e. the length of a bunk. The 13-ft main cabin may still be introduced in either the motor or sailing yacht, but a web frame, of perhaps 8-in depth in the case of GRP construction, should be fitted between bulkheads. GRP design has led to sloppiness in attitudes towards structural considerations. For example, it has recently been the tendency for some owners to employ interior designers without appropriate training to design the internal arrangements. This can have disastrous effects on the structural integrity of the vessel if the internal arrangements designer does not consult the naval architect. The GRP yacht hull is delivered normally through the fitting-out yard with all structural bulkheads laminated to the hull in positions according to the naval architect's drawings; access openings are then cut in these bulkheads where required, and the accommodation fitted between. As mentioned it is often possible to remove most of the bulkhead, provided a web frame of perhaps 8-in depth is left attached to the hull. This might require additional laminating to improve its strength. In cases where the internal arrangements designer has asked for some of the bulkheads to be completely removed or doorways cut to the full depth of the shell, the hull has suffered later from excessive deflection or distortion, or worse, from doors not closing, joinery opening at corners or even crazing and cracks appearing in the shell. There is much to be said for the strength exhibited in many of the older racing yachts, though lacking the bright, open decor of many of their flimsy modern counterparts.

Overcrowding is becoming a particularly difficult problem in certain areas, and antipollution laws have been introduced in some countries prohibiting the pumping of raw sewage into harbours and marinas. In most good marinas there is no necessity to use toilets aboard as adequate shore facilities are provided. However, these laws have led to the incorporation of sewage or holdover tanks into yachts' tankage systems, even though it is often very difficult to provide sufficient tankage for the sailing yacht with the fin and skeg configuration, as most of the underfloor room is used for fuel and water. WCs and sinks have outlets to the holdover tank which is then periodically pumped into a shore sewer. This whole system is often tedious, inconvenient and time-consuming, particularly when cruising in inland waterways with several people aboard. The answer lies in the development of miniature sewage treating systems, so that harmless liquids may be pumped directly from the yacht in small quantities. This could be effected by decomposition of the harmful or unpleasant sewage products by bacteria or chemicals, and mechanical separation of a large percentage of the water from the tank, enabling a more concentrated liquid to remain, thus greatly extending the carrying capacity without having to use all available space for holdover tanks. If sewage is left in a holdover tank for any period of time without chemical treatment to prevent decomposition, pressure will build up with the formation of unpleasant gases. A vent pipe should be fitted, with outlet below the waterline, and bent in a U to prevent leakage, to allow these gases to escape. Where possible, holdover tanks should be made of plastic, as sewage products and soaps are very corrosive, even to stainless and galvanised steels, over a period of time.

Heating and air conditioning methods play an important role in the increase in comfort on board, particularly where yachts have to operate in tropical climates or where there are extreme temperatures during day and night. Most seafaring people realise that insulation to prevent condensation is one of the most important contributors to comfort. Some vessels are not just damp inside due to deck leaks, but wet right through due to excessive condensation caused by lack of insulation between the cold exterior and the warm interior. This is prevalent in hulls built of material having a high thermal conductivity such as steel and aluminium. The problem is not so acute in wood and ferrocement due to lower conductivity and the much thicker shell, and in GRP, sandwich decks are usually adopted. The best insulating material is non-flammable or, if the polyurethane or PVC foams are used, a fire retardant or non-inflammable skin should be coated over the surface. This can be done by laminating a heavy woven roving over the foam, using if possible an intumescent polyester (that is a polyester which swells on heating forming a sort of fireproof blanket). In the future semi-rigid foam insulating materials should become available with a variety of flameproof surfaces in imitation leather and cloth textures. It would then be possible to unroll the material and glue it to the yacht's side, eliminating the need for the fairing and covering of the foam. Condensation can be overcome further with the use of extensive heating and air conditioning incorporating dehumidifiers.

In the case of large motor yachts it is possible to run the engine cooling water under the cabin sole through an extensive network of piping acting as radiators, so that no additional heating is required under normal temperature operating conditions. At present little attention is given to the recycling of the heat energy put into engine cooling water.

Plastics have permitted far more exotic house and office furniture to be designed. Yet the designing of most bunks and seats in yachts has been approached with a traditional outlook, as it is often felt that traditional wooden designs are more seamanlike. There is no reason why more stylish furniture should not be incorporated which could be built of GRP formers to the required shape, covered in sponge rubber and an easily cleaned plastic or leathercloth finish. It may be regarded as safer for those inside the yacht under severe conditions, for if all the hard edges and corners of traditional construction are dispensed with the likelihood of injury is lessened. This modern outlook to internal design should not be confused with the important feature mentioned earlier: that all the structural bulkheads and floors should be initially built into the yacht, making the hull as rigid as necessary prior to fitting furniture.

Much of the criticism of plastic internal mouldings and furnishings has arisen because the builder has been unimaginative in his outlook on colour and texture of finish. Normally, a harsh white or perhaps blue is adopted in a smooth gloss finish. But there is no reason why leather-cloth or perhaps a mosaic pattern should not be incorporated in the surface of the mould, and with the huge selection of colours available for gel coat finish a modern but extremely pleasing decor could be produced at very little difference in cost. It is often felt that the only way to obtain a warm and pleasing look in plastics is to imitate wood; this is far from the truth, as with careful selection of texture and colour the whole arrangement in plastic can be both modern and tasteful. Generally, far more thought is put into the very expensive one-off yacht, but for the series production type (although costing up to four or five years' pay for the owner) one has to select from what is on the market. Thus, it is left to builders to make changes in standard specifications, and to take the trouble to know what materials are available and at what extra cost.

One exciting innovation in domestic design has been inflatable furniture. It should be adopted in yacht design where either weight or room has strict limitations. With a small air compressor aboard and inflatable bunks fastened along the side shelf, the hull interior may be made much lighter and more open during the daytime when the bunks are not required. This furniture has superb insulating qualities and is very comfortable. The main objection is that it is possible to puncture the material, causing an embarrassing letdown at night! However, plastic coated nylon materials are strong and unlikely to puncture. This inflatable technique can be applied to non-structural partitions which can be erected at a press of the compressor switch when privacy between cabins is required. An interesting arrangement is shown where a very large open cabin adopted during the day in the sailing yacht permits a numerous crew to sit round in comfort in harbour, or allows easier access to sail bins while racing, at a much reduced structure weight; the hull is stiffened throughout by web frames and partition bulkheads may be inflated to form the partitions (Fig. 8.2).

In GRP construction the naval architect not only produces line drawings of the hull shape, but also of the deck and superstructure, if these are moulded using complex curves, and of the internal moulding if it is complex. This involves considerably more work than in the design of the traditional wooden yacht, for both sail and power. All too often it is left to the loftsman of the moulding yard to try to determine the shape of a complex superstructure from a profile and perhaps a section drawing. This imposes a serious and unfair responsibility on the yard and may lead to a sour relationship between yard and designer, particularly if the final shape of the yacht is not what the naval architect had in mind.

When designing the complex internal mouldings it is preferable to have the minimum number of moulds necessary to release the shape, as mould lining-up and bolting time is valuable moulding time lost, particularly if a high output from a set of moulds is required. A minimum moulding release angle of 2° between faces is desirable (Fig. 8.3). Otherwise the moulding may easily become locked in and be damaged when forcing a release. Often small star fractures in the gel coat can be observed along vertical faces of a complex moulding where the mould had been banged in an attempt to release the moulding. The designer should know that GRP shrinks on curing, which may lead to either the mould locking or the gel coat drawing away from the mould surface in certain internal moulding complex shapes, causing an unfair patch in an otherwise smooth surface. Care should be taken to avoid deep channels when designing the mouldings for GRP; this often arises in way of cockpit coamings and

Fig. 8.2. General arrangement with inflatable furniture. During the daytime the inflatable bunks and partitions are stowed to provide a large open cabin area.

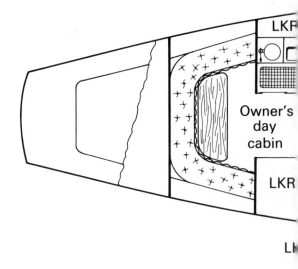

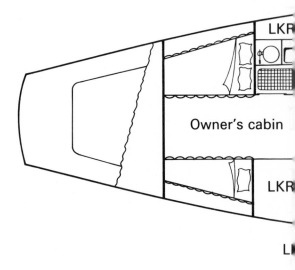

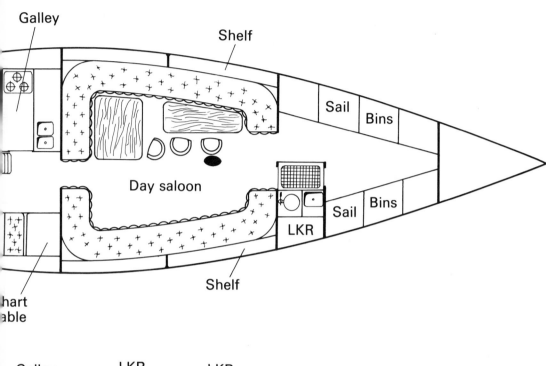

Galley

Shelf

Sail

Bins

Day saloon

Sail

Bins

LKR

Shelf

hart
ble

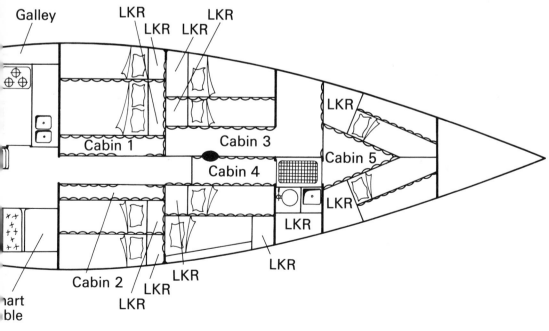

Galley

LKR

LKR

LKR

LKR

LKR

Cabin 1

Cabin 3

Cabin 5

Cabin 4

LKR

Cabin 2

LKR

LKR

LKR

LKR

LKR

hart
ble

Fig. 8.3. Release angle diagram. Drawing showing the
required 2° release angle on the mould.

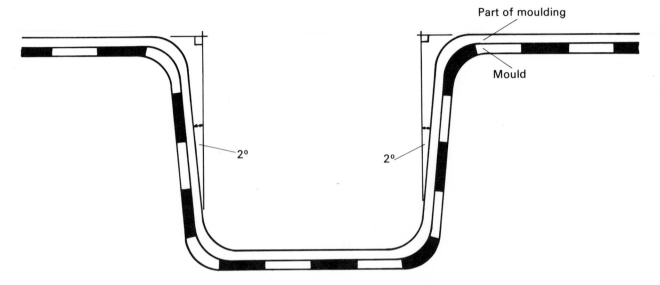

fronts. Deep channels are awkward for laminaters
when rolling out the glass. Thus many air voids will
be left between the gel coat and the first layer of
chopped strand mat which, after a few years' service,
will result in the gel coat-being knocked in way of the
voids, causing a collapse and an ugly hollow.

With the high cost of plug building and mould
construction it is possible to design the internal
mould to fit a whole range of craft. For instance, a
standard bathroom moulding incorporating toilet
pedestal, sink, shelf, cupboard and shower basin
could be used in a whole range of craft, both sail and
power. Also, parts of a mould may be used,
eliminating the building of a whole new plug. For
example, on a 45-ft sailing yacht some owners might
require a flush deck for racing giving easy access and
a large working platform for the crew, while others
might prefer a coachroof and wheelhouse for
cruising comfort. For the latter, the outside of the
flush deck mould may be utilised to laminate the
cruising yacht deck as far as the coachroof and
wheelhouse.

In Chapter 3 it was seen that suspension of the
internal structure can be adopted to lessen the g load
on the helmsmen of high-speed motor yachts,
particularly for power-boat racing. Although this
system requires extensive research into the most
suitable system of springs and dampers, it is worth
considering for any type of motor yacht, to give a
more comfortable ride in short head sea conditions.
This could be a standard feature in yacht design of
the future, for perhaps yachts are at a stage of
development equivalent to cars in the early 1900s,
giving a bone-shaking ride at speed without any form
of suspension. One only has to see how automobile
suspension has developed over the past seventy
years to realise what advances can be made. The
system would have the greatest advantage in the
most expensive yachts, particularly the fast motor
yacht, where comfort usually is a secondary
consideration to speed. Although additional weight
would be incurred by fitting springs and dampers,
the pressure loading on the hull bottom plate during
impact is lessened, as the weight of the hull in total is

decelerated over a longer period. Thus the hull shell scantlings may be reduced.

The lighting of yacht interiors has undergone steady change over the past twenty years. The standard form of lighting was the oil lamp, awkward to use because of the smoke and smell and very wasteful of energy, as most of that produced is heat. Following this, bottled-gas lighting arrived. It gave a much brighter light without the soot and smell of the oil lamps; however, it had its own disadvantages like the possibility of explosion if a leak should occur in the piping system, and the fragile mantle which lasted only for two or three weeks. Incandescent lamps consisting of the normal hot-filament wire was the next development and these are fitted to the majority of yachts built today. They have the disadvantage that they draw a heavy current from the battery storage for the amount of light emitted. Also they require well-insulated wiring from the battery, for salt water is such a corrosive agent and conductor that the battery can be easily discharged if an electrical breakdown should occur.

The latest development is the 12 V fluorescent light which emits a large percentage of its energy in the form of light, being nearly ten times more efficient in production of light than the incandescent lamp. However, the inverter necessary to convert the low-voltage supply into the high voltage necessary to fire the tube requires careful insulation against moisture, and incandescent lamps should not be adopted at the chart table for DF radio due to interference of the fluorescent type on radio equipment.

The future is likely to bring about glowing panels of semiconducting materials such as gallium arsenide, which could be energised from the 12 V battery system. Experiments in this field indicate low current consumption for the candlepower emitted, enabling the lighting to be used for long periods of time without draining the batteries. Subtle changes in the voltage input to the semiconductor result in a variation in colour, and the lighting could be dimmed as well. These panels might even be connected to the output of the stereo or quadrophonic system giving a complete psychedelic display!

Electronic aids to navigation such as radio direction finding, anemometers, echosounders, ship-to-shore-telephone and radars are among the items which have allowed navigation to assume greater accuracy and ease. Over the past four years the size and cost of radars has steadily decreased, and this is a trend that will continue, so that, within ten years, it will be possible to mount the radar transmission and receiving aerial and electronics inside a dome the size of a football. A radar this size could be gyroscopically mounted, enabling the heel and motion of the yacht to be eliminated from the emitter–receiver. A new development in radar technology for the yachtsman is the introduction of 'passive radar'. This picks up the X-band or radar band transmission of about 9,000–11,500 MHz from other vessels. This detector is highly directional and thus gives the relative direction and distance of the transmitting vessel. If one finds the bearing is constant and range closing, the boat is on a collision course. This system could be coupled to an alarm so that in fog the helmsman could be warned of impending collision.

Speed logs have undergone an interesting development with the introduction of the Doppler effect log. This dispenses with the old mechanical impeller or pressure tubes and operates by sending out a signal ahead of the yacht, most of which is dissipated in the sea, with a small part reflected back from the still water ahead of and below the yacht. The returned wave is compared electronically with the emitted wave and thus the speed of the vessel over the ground is automatically deduced.

Probably the potentially most dangerous item used on board is bottled gas. It is heavier than air, and if a leak occurs it will drain into the bilges. Sparks in that area, for instance from the engine starter motor commutator, will cause an explosion. In such an explosion the whole deck and deckhouse of a 50-ft yacht can be blown off the hull. Gas detectors have been available for several years but they were usually based on hot-wire conduction. The latest type incorporates semiconductor sensors which are less likely to fail and give a more positive reading. But still one of the safest ways to avoid such a gas buildup is to run an air-extraction pump with its inlet placed in the bilge. This could be used in conjunction with the bilge pump so that initially all the bilge water is extracted, then the air above this water is removed, allowing fresh air to take its place. Prevention is better than cure, and a gas tight locker with drain overboard should be adopted where possible.

Echosounders have been available to the yachtsman for many years now. These provide one of the most useful tools for navigation. The development changes tend to be in detail rather than in the system. They consist of a pulse generator working in the range of 20 to 150 kHz while a transducer often bolted to the bottom of the boat converts this electrical pulse to sound waves directed at the sea bed. The signal is returned to the transducer receiver and is electronically converted to show the depth below the yacht's bottom. The nature of the sea bed can be indicated by the type of pulse, as a smooth rock or sand bed gives a sharp narrow pulse, a muddy bed is indicated by a broad less intense pulse, and an uneven, rocky bed gives a split pulse. Developments in transducer receivers could enable this part of the equipment to be mounted inside the hull on gimbals, eliminating the necessity to cut a hole in the bottom of a GRP or wood yacht, and also removing the problem sometimes experienced of weak signal, when the sailing yacht is heeled well over.

Semi-conductor and integrated circuit technology will allow these developments to take place with greater reliability and with systems occupying smaller areas. This is particularly true of radar and radio telephone. And, of course, the cost of these items should decrease steadily as semi-conductor manufacture is developed – a pleasing thought for all yachtsmen!

References

Alexander, W. and Street, A. *Metals in the Service of Man* 6th edition. Harmondsworth, Middlesex: Penguin 1969

Allen, H. G. *Analysis and Design of Structural Sandwich Panels*. Oxford: Pergamon 1969

Du Caine, P. *High Speed Small Craft* 2nd edition. London: Temple Press 1956

Fox, U. *Seamanlike Sense in Powercraft*. London: Peter Davies 1968

Eagle, M. W. *Flying Ships: Hovercraft and Hydrofoils*. New York: Dodd Mead 1970

Johnson, P. *Yachtsman's Guide to the Rating Rule*. Lymington, Hants: Nautical Publishing 1971

Levi, R. *Dhows to Deltas*. Lymington, Hants: Nautical Publishing 1971

Mandel, P. *Water, Air and Interface Vehicles*. Cambridge, Mass: MIT Press 1969

Marchaj, C. A. *Sailing Theory and Practice*. London: Adlard Coles 1964

Polyester Handbook. Northamptonshire: Scott Bader & Company Ltd 1967

Simmons, C. R. *Gas Turbine Manual* 3rd edition. London: Temple Press 1968

Skene, N. L. *Elements of Yacht Design* 2nd edition ed. F. S. Kinney and D. P. Birt. London: Black 1963

Index